JACK THE RIPPER
AND
THE EAST END

JACK THE RIPPER
AND
THE EAST END

With an introduction
by

Peter Ackroyd

Compiled and edited
by

Alex Werner

CHATTO & WINDUS
in association with
THE MUSEUM IN DOCKLANDS
& MUSEUM OF LONDON

Published by Chatto & Windus
in association with the Museum in Docklands & Museum of London

2 4 6 8 10 9 7 5 3 1

Copyright © 2008 Museum of London
Introduction copyright © 2008 Peter Ackroyd
While copyright in the volume as a whole is vested in the Museum of London, copyright in individual
chapters belongs to their respective authors, and no chapter may be reproduced wholly or in part without
the express permission in writing of both author and the Museum of London

Peter Ackroyd and the Museum of London have asserted their right under the Copyright,
Designs and Patents Act 1988 to be identified as the authors of this work

This book is sold subject to the condition that it shall not, by way of trade or otherwise,
be lent, resold, hired out, or otherwise circulated without the publisher's prior consent in any form
of binding or cover other than that in which it is published and without a similar condition,
including this condition, being imposed on the subsequent purchaser

First published in Great Britain in 2008 by
Chatto & Windus
Random House, 20 Vauxhall Bridge Road,
London SW1V 2SA

www.rbooks.co.uk

Addresses for companies within The Random House Group Limited
can be found at: www.randomhouse.co.uk/offices.htm

The Random House Group Limited Reg. No. 954009

A CIP catalogue record for this book is available from the British Library

ISBN 9780701182472

Endpapers: *Detail from Charles Booth's hand-coloured* Map of Poverty, c.*1888–9.*

Frontispiece: *The Whitechapel Murders were reported throughout the world.*
Here, an engraving from the French magazine Le Journal Illustré *shows the discovery of what was
described as the '10th victim'. On 13 February 1891 Frances Coles was brutally murdered in Swallow Gardens,
Royal Mint Street in Whitechapel. Although over two years after the murders of 1888, the event
was quickly identified in the popular press as being the work of Jack the Ripper.*

Mixed Sources
Product group from well-managed
forests and other controlled sources
www.fsc.org Cert no. TT-COC-2139
© 1996 Forest Stewardship Council
FSC

The Random House Group Limited supports the Forest Stewardship Council (FSC),
the leading international forest certification organisation. All our titles that are printed on
Greenpeace approved FSC certified paper carry the FSC logo. Our paper procurement
policy can be found at www.rbooks.co.uk/environment

Book design by Peter Ward
Printed and bound in Great Britain by
Butler & Tanner, Frome, Somerset

CONTENTS

JACK THE RIPPER AND THE EAST END

P ETER A CKROYD

They are the most infamous murders in British history, the solution to which has baffled social historians and criminologists for over a century. On Friday, 31 August 1888, the body of a woman was found in Buck's Row, Whitechapel. Her name was Mary Ann Nichols, and her throat had been cut. A prostitute living in a doss-house, she was desperately looking for custom. 'I'll soon get my money,' she told the doss-house keeper. 'See what a jolly bonnet I have.' Eight days later the body of another prostitute, Annie May Chapman, was found in Hanbury Street in the same neighbourhood of Spitalfields. Annie Chapman was lying on her back with her legs

Three East End women, c.1900

Jack the Ripper's victims were largely women in their late thirties or early forties.
At the coroner's inquests the description of their appearance and the second-hand clothes that they
wore reflected their poverty. Despite everything, they were proud women, especially of their new
bonnets and ribbons. Spitalfields and Whitechapel attracted many women who had fallen on hard
times. In order to pay for their lodging and support their addiction to drink and tobacco they often
resorted to prostitution. During the day, they would sleep on park benches and in alleyways.
Some tried to earn a living by hawking goods at street markets.

spread wide. The coroner noted that the body had been 'terribly mutilated' and that the throat had been deeply cut with the thin narrow blade of a very sharp knife, not dissimilar to one used by surgeons.

On 30 September the murderer claimed two more victims, Elizabeth Stride and Catherine Eddowes; their bodies were found in the neighbouring parishes of St-George's-in-the-East and Aldgate. Elizabeth Stride, unlike the other victims, was not mutilated; only her throat was cut. Catherine Eddowes was less fortunate; the coroner, who came upon the body within half an hour of the murder, reported that

> the intestines were drawn out to a large extent and placed over the right shoulder – they were smeared over with some feculent matter. A piece of about two feet was quite detached from the body and placed between the body and the left arm, apparently by design. The lobe and auricle of the right ear were cut obliquely through.

'Feculent' here is derived from faeces.

On the night of this double discovery, a message was written in chalk on the wall of a nearby street reading '*The Juwes are the men That Will not be Blamed for nothing*'; beside the writing was a piece of the apron of Catherine Eddowes. There had been talk in the neighbourhood that the crimes were the work of a Jew known colloquially as 'Leather Apron'. A police superintendent ordered that the offending words should be erased.

A fifth victim, Mary Jane Kelly, was found on 9 November, lying on the bed of the room which she rented; her lodgings were in Spitalfields, the area in which the first killing had occurred. Her body had been terribly mutilated, with various organs strewn across the room, and her face slashed beyond recognition. Certain neighbours had recalled a cry of 'murder!', but in the East End such cries were frequent enough to be disregarded.

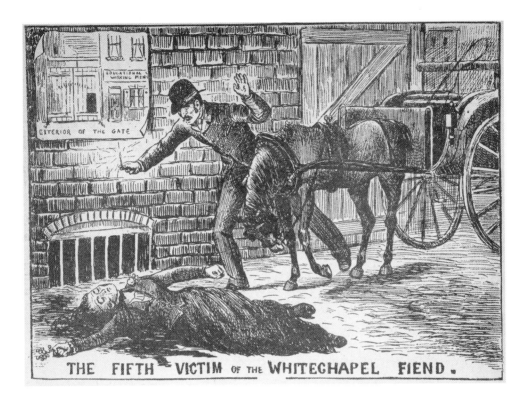

THE FIFTH VICTIM OF THE WHITECHAPEL FIEND.

In this wood engraving from the Illustrated Police News *of 6 October 1888 Louis Diemschutz discovers the body of Elizabeth Stride in Dutfield Yard, just off Berner Street. He was the steward of the International Working Men's Educational Club which backed on to the yard.*

There had been other murders linked to these most notorious crimes. In the spring of 1888 a prostitute named Emma Smith was assaulted in Osborne Street, Whitechapel, where her right ear was torn and a blunt instrument of some kind inserted into her stomach. She died later in the London Hospital. Then on 7 August, three weeks before the murder of Mary Ann Nichols, Martha Tabram was found lying dead in a pool of her own blood on a first-floor landing in Whitechapel. She had been stabbed thirty-nine times.

Later in that year, after the killing of Mary Jane Kelly, a prostitute was strangled in Poplar. The police surgeon in the case is quoted as saying that it was the handiwork of the 'Whitechapel fiend'. In the following year two other women were found foully mutilated, Ripper-fashion, in Whitechapel and in the nearby parish of St-George's-in-the-East. Then, on 13 February 1891, the body of a woman was discovered in an alley that ran beneath the railway arches in Whitechapel. Her throat had been slashed from side to side with such violence that she was almost decapitated. So ended the killings that were soon ascribed to an anonymous murderer for ever after known as 'Jack the Ripper'. The 'Whitechapel Murders', as they were originally known, became for posterity the 'Ripper Murders'.

The name was taken from an anonymous letter sent to the police on 25 September. It exulted in the murders. '*I am down on whores,*' it said, '*and I shant quit ripping them till I do get buckled.*' It is still not clear whether this communication was or was not a hoax. A more noisome missive was received by a member of the Whitechapel Vigilance Committee in the middle of October. Half of a human kidney had been placed in a box. One of the kidneys of Catherine Eddowes had been removed by the killer. In an accompanying letter the writer claimed to have '*fried and ate*' the missing portion, and that it had been '*very nise*'. This may have been the work of a medical student engaging in a prank. Such informative details, however, may have led the way to such notorious fictional killers as Hannibal Lecter.

There have been many theories about the identity of the real man known as Jack the Ripper, the candidates for this honour including Walter Sickert; Prince Albert Victor 'Eddy', the Duke of Clarence; and a royal physician called Sir William Gull. Less prominent men have been chosen as the perpetrators, among them two doctors and a barrister. None of the identifications is convincing. Conspiracy theories also abound but, like most conspiracy theories, they come to nothing.

Detail of Dear Boss letter, 25 September 1888

A number of letters by the 'supposed' killer were sent to news agencies and the police. Some offered advice and hints to where the murderer would next strike, others made fun of the police and their attempts to catch him. Most, if not all, of the letters were considered to be hoaxes at the time. On 27 September 1888, the 'Dear Boss' letter, in horrific red ink, was received by the Central News Agency. The writer signs off the letter 'Jack the Ripper' – the first time that the name had appeared in writing or print. It is possible that the name was already in use on the streets of Whitechapel and Spitalfields. The name Jack had been used earlier in the Victorian period to describe another mysterious attacker – 'Spring-heeled Jack', a devil-like figure who jumped over walls and frightened unsuspecting Londoners.

FINDING THE MUTILATED BODY IN MITRE SQARE

The body of Catherine Eddowes was discovered by Constable Watkins of the City of London Police Force at around 1.45 a.m. on 30 September 1888. He explained to the coroner and jury at the Eddowes inquest that his patrol or beat took between 12 and 14 minutes and at 1.30 a.m. there had been nothing that 'had excited his attention' in Mitre Square.

The real significance of the sequence of crimes lies elsewhere. It lies in the locality of the murders, known generally if somewhat inaccurately as 'the East End'. One of the crimes actually took place in the City of London. But it was the East that took on the burden of mystery and criminality. It was the East that was seen as the harbinger of death and decay.

The press of the time prompted that hysterical response. The crimes of Jack the Ripper did not herald the birth of 'tabloid' journalism – that was already latent in the pamphlets of the seventeenth and eighteenth centuries – but the salacious reporting of sensational events became imprinted in the public consciousness as a result of the events of the autumn and winter of 1888. It was the most lurid of all press seasons. 'Every new turn of this bewildering labyrinth', the *Star* wrote on 14 September, 'reveals some fresh depth of social blackness, some strange and repulsive curiosity of human nature. What are we to do? Where are we to turn?' The newspapers were filled with headlines and horrors. 'GHASTLY MURDER IN THE EAST END', one front page informed its readers. 'DREAD-FUL MUTILATION OF A WOMAN'. Fanciful illustrations and drawings abounded. This was an era when a new reading public was being formed, and it is possible to define this storm of comment and controversy as the true birth of what has become known as the popular

Advert for Hudson's soap, *Graphic*, 1 December 1888
During the hunt for the Whitechapel Murderer, the question of offering a reward for catching the killer loomed large. Here, an enterprising advertiser promoting Hudson's soap has reworked the popular iconography of the policeman and his bull's-eye lamp.

press. The potent combination of sexuality and criminality was too tempting to be resisted, and so the East End became generally depicted as the heart of darkness. The phrase itself, 'East End', was not invented until this decade.

SUSPICIOUS CHARACTERS

In the autumn of 1888, the newspapers began to speculate about the identity of the killer. From witness statements, descriptions were prepared and circulated to police forces and indirectly to the public through the press.

'Age 37; height, 5ft. 7in.; rather dark beard and moustache. Dress-shirt, dark vest and trousers, black scarf, and black felt hat. Spoke with a foreign accent'.

The police were active in following up various leads but to no avail. One prime suspect emerged known as Leather Apron. The *Star* newspaper revealed that he carried 'a razor-

like knife', threatened to 'rip up' women and was able to 'move noiselessly' around the streets of Whitechapel and Spitalfields. Named as John Pizer, a Polish Jew and boot finisher who regularly wore a leather apron and lived in lodging-houses in the area, he was held by the police for questioning but released when his alibi was established. In the search for the killer, the focus of the police and media ranged widely from soldiers to horse slaughterers, from lascar seamen to medical students. Such was the mania that even George R. Sims (*pictured left*), the popular writer and journalist, while reporting the story, was mistakenly identified by a coffee stall keeper as the murderer. He bore a resemblance to a mysterious blood-stained customer on the night of the double

Jack the Ripper as depicted in the silent film Waxworks *(1924).*

Two sketches of the murderer, Illustrated Police News, *20 October 1888.*

murder. Sims writing many years later explained that the murderer was 'undoubtedly a doctor who had been in a lunatic asylum and had developed homicidal mania of a special kind'.

Surviving archive reveals that detectives had at least five possible suspects. One was Francis Tumblety, a 'quack' doctor who had a collection of uteri. He was arrested for homosexual practices but escaped to the United States while on bail. Another was Montague Druitt, a barrister and schoolmaster, who committed suicide not long after Mary Kelly's death. Attention was given also to Aaron Kosminski, a Jewish barber, who had a 'great hatred of women' and 'strong homicidal tendencies' and to George Chapman (also known as Klosowski), another barber who was hanged in 1905. Another suspect was Michael Ostrog, a Russian doctor and a convict who was subsequently detained in a lunatic asylum as a homicidal maniac.

Since the Second World War, speculation about the killer's identity has proliferated.

Perhaps the most sensational is the Royal Conspiracy theory that claims that Prince Albert Victor, the Duke of Clarence (*pictured right*), one of Queen Victoria's grandsons, carried out the murders having become insane through contracting syphilis. He was, also, linked to the Cleveland Street male brothel affair. Another version maintains that Sir William Gull, a Freemason, was the killer, acting on behalf of senior government figures and members of the Royal family to cover up for the Prince's indiscretions. The killings were thought to be part of an elaborate Masonic ritual.

Walter Sickert, the painter, was named as an accomplice to the murders in the Royal Conspiracy theory. Soon, some writers were claiming that he was the murderer. James Maybrick became a suspect with the publication of a diary where he confessed to being the killer. Recently, Joseph Silver, a Polish Jew, has been promoted as a contender as well as Melville McNaghten, the Assistant Chief Constable appointed after the murders. It has even been suggested that Jack the Ripper was in fact Jill the Ripper. To avoid suspicion and detection, disguised as midwife, the killer would have been able to carry out the murders more easily. It is perhaps worth noting that Sir Arthur Conan Doyle, the creator of Sherlock Holmes, was one of the proposers of this theory.

Sir William Gull

Walter Sickert

James Maybrick

Yet the excoriation of the East represented an old tradition of superstition. The conquering Saxons of the tenth century resided on the west side of the River Walbrook, while the vanquished Britons were consigned to the east side of the territory. The taint of poverty, already evident in the medieval period, was memorialised by John Stow in his *Survey of London*; he observed that in the east of London there was a 'continual street or filthy strait passage with alleys of small tenements or cottages built almost to Ratcliffe'. Ratcliff is now part of the Borough of Stepney. By the end of the sixteenth century the whole area was being described as 'base' and 'filthy'. In 1665 Spitalfields, the neighbourhood of the first and last murders by Jack the Ripper, was reported to be inhabited by 'poor indigent and idle and loose persons'. Such were the 'persons', of course, who were murdered two centuries later. The small industries of the neighbourhood were filthy, too, banished from the rest of London. In the early 1660s Sir William Petty, an economist and statistician, lamented 'the fumes, steams and stinks of the whole Easterly Pyle'.

So in the seventeenth and eighteenth centuries the movement of the genteel and the aspiring Londoner was towards the West. The West End became the centre of luxury and of conspicuous consumption. The western neighbourhoods were laid out in fashionable squares and avenues. Here grew up Mayfair and Belgravia, Knightsbridge and Chelsea. In the East lay Spitalfields and Whitechapel and Wapping, all of them bywords for corruption and criminality. The West End had the money, and the East End had the dirt.

☞ From the Poultry to Bishopsgate Street and to Whitechapel, 1889
This bird's-eye view shows Whitechapel's proximity to the banking halls and exchanges of the City of London where financial deals were struck and world prices fixed. Will Crooks, a local politician, questioned how was it that the sun that never set on the British Empire never rose on the dark alleys of the East End.

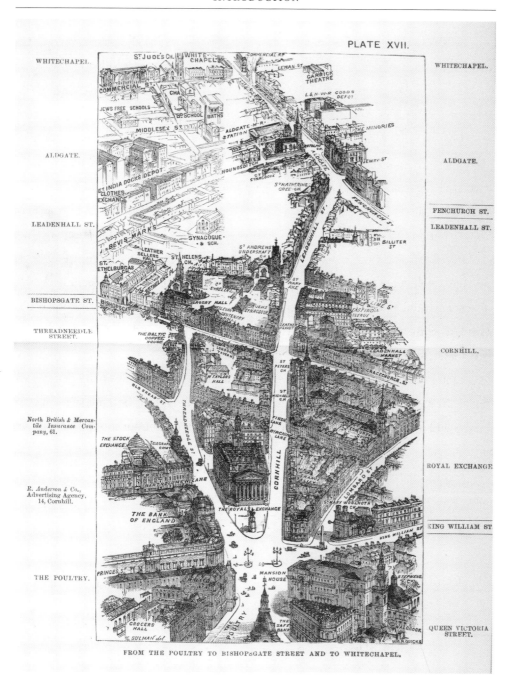

PLATE XVII.

FROM THE POULTRY TO BISHOPSGATE STREET AND TO WHITECHAPEL.

All these unsavoury features became more and more prominent in the course of the nineteenth century. The East became an unwitting or unwilling agent of the Industrial Revolution, when such heavy working districts as Canning Town and Silvertown were created. The River Lea, once the crystal-bright stream of Spenser's poetry, became the site of 'stink industries' such as tanning and dyeing. The East End became the area where the maximum number of people were herded into the smallest possible space.

'Pyle' was one word for the East End. It was also known as the 'wen' and the 'sink'. In the 1880s, as a direct result of the Ripper murders, it became known as 'the abyss'. It became notorious as the haven of immorality and evil and savagery. In the decades after the Ripper killings there was a plethora of studies with titles such as *The People of the Abyss*, *The Nether World*, *In Darkest London* and *The Black Stain*. In *The Nether World* George Gissing invoked 'the pest-stricken regions of East London, sweltering in sunshine which served only to reveal the intimacies of abomination'. This was the region where Oscar Wilde dispatched Dorian Gray for nights of opium and, perhaps, unnamed vice; this was the region where rose the evil genius of Fu Manchu. 'The East' became a token of that large and menacing 'East' that lay beyond the boundaries of Christian Europe. That is why the poverty-stricken children of the East End became known as 'street-Arabs'.

Wentworth Street, Whitechapel, Gustave Doré, 1872

Douglas Jerrold, in his text accompanying Doré's illustrations, described the proximity of the wealthy financial markets of the City of London to those at its eastern edge. He viewed the latter as 'picturesque' with 'the overhanging clothes, the mounds of vegetables, the piles of hardware, the confused heaps of fish, all cast about to catch the pence of the bonnetless dishevelled women, the heavy navvies, and the shoeless children'.

Photographs of shoeless and poorly clothed East End children were used by organisations such as the Salvation Army and other Christian missions to raise money. Dr Barnado became active in ragged schools and Christian missions after encountering Jim Jarvis, a young 'street arab', who took him on a nocturnal tour of Whitechapel where he was shown the alleys and rooftops where the street children slept.

Offering food and shelter to poor homeless children was thought by some to encourage
idleness and begging. On 17 November 1888, a piece in the Daily Telegraph *urged that*
'any assistance should be directed, not to casual help, but to permanent elevation'.
It went on: 'Find out why the boy or girl is destitute. Trace them to their homes. If the parent
is neglectful either through drunkenness or hardness of heart, summon him to a police-court,
get him punished, and send the child to a reformatory, making the father pay
for its maintenance if he can afford it.'

Whitechapel and Spitalfields had always been a home of immigrant populations, too, further emphasising the exotic nature of their communities. The '*Juwes*' had been singled out by the anonymous writer of the chalk message because the Jews maintained a large presence in the immediate neighbourhood. It has been suggested that the words '*Will not be Blamed for nothing*' was a Cockney way of saying that they will not take responsibility for anything. It was a Cockney double negative, in other words. It was, perhaps, the work of a disgruntled or simply xenophobic native. Spitalfields had originally been the home of Huguenots; then it was settled by the Irish; then it became the centre of Jewish immigration; in the late twentieth century it has become a haven for the Bangladeshis and Somalis. If there is a spirit of place here, it is one of endless change and dispossession.

Yet there was one salutary response to the Ripper killings. Several of the newspapers at the time, incensed at the conditions of dirt and danger that the murders revealed, led an active campaign to alleviate the poverty and the insanitary state of the East End. It was believed that the unhappy conditions of the area actively promoted crime, if not perhaps on the scale that the Ripper had executed. So there were efforts to remove the worst effects of indigence. George Bernard Shaw, in a letter at the time, noted that

> while we social democrats were wasting our time on education, agitation and organization, some independent genius has taken the matter in hand, and by simply murdering and disembowelling four women, converted the proprietary press to an inept sort of communism.

The ensuing philanthropic work was not entirely new. In the 1860s various halls and chapels had been erected in the East End to promote charitable work among the poor. Yet the Ripper murders were the context, if not the inspiration, for the growth of 'missions' in the impoverished streets of Stepney or Whitechapel, and Arnold

Newspaper delivery horse and cart, Farringdon Road, *c.*1900
The Star *evening newspaper's office was in Stonecutter's Street, near Farringdon Road,*
in the City of London. Launched in January 1888, the Star *soon became one of London's leading*
popular titles and claimed to have the largest circulation of any evening paper in the kingdom.
It reported the Jack the Ripper murders in graphic detail, speculating on the murderer's
identity and criticising the police investigation.

*A crowd of East End onlookers are drawn to a newsagent's window where
the latest issue of the* Illustrated Police News *has been displayed. This weekly
publication depicted in gory detail all the latest murders and crimes.*

Toynbee set up a public library in Whitechapel, also for the benefit of what were then known as the labouring poor.

Yet the East End remained, until the last decades of the twentieth century, a synonym for poverty, and unemployment, and disease. As a result of the five main Ripper murders, Whitechapel and its environs became the shadow line of London. The fact that the murderer was never caught only seemed to confirm the impression that, somehow or other, the streets themselves had perpetrated the crime. The East End was the 'real' Ripper. As a result it became the receptacle for all the anxieties about urban life in general. It became the emblem for the closely packed and anonymous metropolis, with its attendant woes and ills. The city was the dark place divorced from nature and natural feeling.

So the crimes of Jack the Ripper have become part of an endless story. They have attained the status of urban myth, or legend, recycled in any number of novels and films and television programmes. The setting of the East End then becomes an excuse for the exploitation of mystery or of horror, and for the more sentimental versions of psychogeography. There is hardly a week when a new publication does not emerge with a fresh theory or a novel interpretation. There are no fewer than three periodicals devoted to the subject. Any hint of a serial killer has sub-editors reaching for the soubriquet of 'Ripper'. In the popular imagination Jack, whoever he or she is, will live for ever.

CHAPTER ONE

THE IMAGINATIVE GEOGRAPHY OF THE WHITECHAPEL MURDERS

JOHN MARRIOTT

During the series of murders that took place in the latter half of 1888, Whitechapel was created in the public imagination as a mythical site of Gothic horror, depravity and fearful danger. So powerful was the oxygen of publicity disseminated by a frenzied press, and by rumour and suspicion, that in some respects the myth remains to this day. A certain chill hovers over the complex cultural landscape of contemporary Whitechapel, particularly in those streets seemingly little changed since the nineteenth century.

This matter raises a number of historical questions of a specific and more general interest. The ready association between Whitechapel and intense public anxiety was by no means inevitable. Over the years many such violent murders occurred in the streets and houses of London without attracting undue interest. Some such as the

Turn him out! – Radcliff. Gustave Doré, 1872

Illustrations in magazines, newspapers and books shaped the public's perception of the East End. Gustave Doré's engravings in London, a Pilgrimage *(1872) were the most influential and ranged widely from the docks and riverside warehouses to the streets and alleys of Whitechapel.*

Ratcliff Highway murders, 1811
The most brutal and horrific East London murders of the early nineteenth century were two related incidents that took place at Ratcliff and Wapping. A total of seven people were murdered and a witness saw two men killing Mrs Williamson and her maid at the King's Arms in New Gravel Lane. A possible suspect, John Williams, a seaman, was found hanged in Coldbath Field prison.

London Monster series of 1788–90 and the Ratcliff Highway murders of 1811 created a deep sense of dread at the time but have not survived in the public imagination except as possible precursors of 1888.[1]

Although there is no conclusive proof of how many of the women who met a violent death in 1888 Whitechapel were murdered by the same person, the mutilation of five East London prostitutes between 31 August and 9 November 1888 provoked an extraordinary panic, and it was around these events that the myth of Whitechapel emerged.[2] So what was it about the area that attracted such interest, how did the murders act as a conduit for a range of intense public anxieties about locality, and precisely how did these concerns feed, and in turn become fed by, specific myths about Whitechapel and the East End more generally towards the close of the nineteenth century? Any satisfying answers to these questions must come from an appreciation of the historical record, particularly in charting change over time. By revealing something of the nature of the distinct imaginative landscapes of east London and the extent to which they are subject to change, we can challenge the mythology of the East End which many of us still inhabit.

WHITECHAPEL AS A LOCALITY

The historical development and identity of east London were shaped by its physical boundaries. The Thames and the Lea were natural, while to the west was the City of London, segregated by an ancient wall. Until the sixteenth century these boundaries had acted as barriers to the expansion of London, but with mounting pressure attendant upon its rise as a great centre of manufacturing, commerce and consumption they became vital arteries. The growth of riverside trades eastwards was forced by the increasingly inadequate port facilities in the centre of the City between London Bridge and the Tower of London. Later the Lea was to kick-start the extraordinary industrialisation of 'London over the border'. The limits imposed by the wall, on the other hand, were rather less natural. The wall was a liminal space between the order and control of the City and an outlying region seemingly beyond the reach of the authority of the City and its livery companies. Here the dead and the dying had been disposed of, and here fledgling trades seeking freedom from restrictive legislation were to seek refuge as the wave of modern metropolitan expansion took off.

Within these boundaries the historical development of east London was structured by highways dating back to Roman times, the most important of which passed from London to Colchester and came to be known as the Whitechapel Road

33

after the name commonly attached to St Mary Matfelon church erected just outside the City wall soon after 1250. This eastern route was for centuries the meeting place of town and country, congested with carts transporting produce and with animals driven to abattoirs. Coaching inns and taverns had been built to cater for this traffic, but by the close of the sixteenth century houses had begun to spread along this and other east-bound thoroughfares, so heralding a transformation in the history of the metropolis. The great surveyor, John Stow, writing in 1598, captured the moment:

> From Aldgate east again lieth a large street, replenished with buildings; to wit, on the north side the parish church of St. Botolph, and so other buildings to Hog Lane, and to the bars on both sides. Also without the bars both the sides of the street be pestered with cottages and alleys, even up to Whitechapel Church, and almost half a mile beyond it, into common field; all which ought to be open and free for all men. But this common field, I say, being sometime the beauty of the city on that part, is so encroached upon by buildings of filthy cottages, and with other purpressors, enclosures, and laystalls (notwithstanding all proclamations and acts of parliament made to the contrary), that in some places it scarce remaineth a sufficient highway for the meeting of carriages and droves of cattle.[3]

From its inception, therefore, Whitechapel seemed to attract a reputation as a site of poverty and lawlessness. Its growth over the next century served only to consolidate its lowly status. The maps of Joel Gascoyne show that by 1703 the old hamlets of east London – Whitechapel, Ratcliff, Limehouse, Spitalfields and Wapping – had emerged as self-contained urban communities, densely packed with intricate networks of courts and alleys close to the main highways.[4] It is not easy to determine precisely why such a topography characterised east London during this formative period. Clearly, the increased population of impoverished riverside and manufacturing labour needed affordable accommodation, but more compelling is the argument that building

A Visit to 'Tiger Bay', *c.*1874

The area just to the north of the St Katharine's Dock and the London Docks and to the south of Whitechapel was known for its disreputable public houses filled with sailors, dock workers, prostitutes and pimps. As James Greenwood related, this was where 'unwary mariners' were 'mercilessly wrecked and stripped and plundered'. Brawling and fighting was the norm. A magistrate was shown an ear that had been 'snapped off a human head by human teeth' in a savage assault.

regulations introduced by Elizabeth to restrict the growth of housing outside London deterred builders from providing decent structures which at a moment's notice could be demolished for infringing the law. These conditions also promoted what was to become one of the most significant social concerns of the next two hundred years, namely, common lodging-houses. As early as 1721 London magistrates denounced the practice in 'the extreme parts of the town' of taking unknown persons into houses for the night on payment of 'one penny or more'.[5] In the course of the century, no doubt facilitated by the large number of derelict houses, lodging-houses increased

THE STRANGERS GUIDE to LONDON

Exhibiting all the various Alterations & Improvements

Edward Mogg's pocket map of 1807 shows the extent of the metropolis. Petticoat Lane marks the eastern boundary of the City of London. Development has spread out beyond the old city walls into Whitechapel and Spitalfields. The London Dock had opened, yet further east there are still fields in Bethnal Green and the area between the Commercial Road and Mile End Road.

dramatically, as did the fear that they provided shelter for the most dissolute and lawless.

The eighteenth-century metropolis witnessed a strong authoritarian impulse to sanitise the more unsightly and dangerous areas through clearance and street-widening schemes. Improvement Acts were first introduced in older City locations, but there soon followed attempts to deal with what were seen to be the deteriorating conditions of the streets of east London. An Act for Better Paving the part of the High Street in the Parish of St Mary Matfelon, otherwise Whitechapel, suggested that the street had been rendered 'incommodious and dangerous to persons passing through' because it was extremely 'ill paved' and 'greatly obstructed by posts and projections . . . and by deep channels'. Commissioners were appointed to undertake the necessary work. There can be little doubt that such Acts did lead to material improvements in the communications infrastructure, but they often came at a high cost. Some twenty years later in neighbouring Spitalfields an improvement Act was passed. Previously commissioners had been empowered to borrow £14,000 to pave parts of Brick Lane but this had proved insufficient, so now they requested powers to borrow more. Interesting also were the misdemeanours identified by the Act in revealing the ongoing struggles between urban authorities committed to good order and an indigenous population clinging resolutely to unruly rural traditions. Penalties were to be exacted for 'slaughtering livestock in the streets, or keeping swine', and wandering cattle would be impounded. Individuals would be prosecuted for 'throwing down dung, dirt, filth, soil or rubbish', or throwing it at 'oranges, or any cock, pigeon, or fowl', as would those who 'shall make or assist in the making of any fire or fires commonly called bonfires, or shall set fire to, or let off, or throw any squib, serpent, rocket, or fireworks whatsoever in any of the said footways or carriage ways'.

Many of the districts so 'improved' had been identified as refuges of the poor and hence criminally minded. Although there were at the time no identifiable working-class districts simply because residential segregation between working-class and middle-class inhabitants had yet to take place, by 1700 distinct enclaves such as the Clink and the Mint in Southwark, Newgate, Spitalfields and Whitechapel were seen to be inhabited by thieves, prostitutes, cheats and beggars who found there spaces remote from the public gaze and defensible against the activities of unwanted intruders.[6] But they were more than that. From these dens sprang the terrifying and mysterious outbreaks of typhus and later cholera which seemed to know no class boundaries, ravaging as they did the ranks of the metropolitan elite as well as the ragged poor. Perhaps most important, these areas were the nuclei of social and political disorder in its various manifestations.

In June 1719 Whitechapel and Spitalfields witnessed riots against the importation of Indian calicoes which were held responsible for the ill-fortunes of local weavers. The riots spread, prompting the Mayor to close the City gate, but were temporarily suspended when troops were sent into Spitalfields. Fearing continued unrest Parliament introduced a bill early in 1720 banning the wearing of calicoes. Its passage, however, was delayed, provoking a further wave of riots until the Act was finally introduced. Defence against unwelcome competition also provoked the anti-Irish riots of 1736 when an estimated 4,000 weavers and other labourers protested against the employment of cheap Irish labour by master weavers in Spitalfields and Whitechapel. The riots spread to other parts of London but all were readily dispersed by the militia. Soon Robert Walpole was able to express relief that the tumults were at an end, and that Jacobite influence had failed to create more general confusion out of a purely Irish affair. Further riots broke out in 1763 and 1768 when looms were smashed and master weavers attacked. The government responded by stationing troops in Spitalfields, and took unprecedentedly draconian action by hanging two leaders of the rioters outside a popular tavern in Bethnal Green. Further riots followed in the ensuing years but they never reached the same level of violence. By then the fate of silk-weaving in east London was sealed as it entered terminal decline.[7]

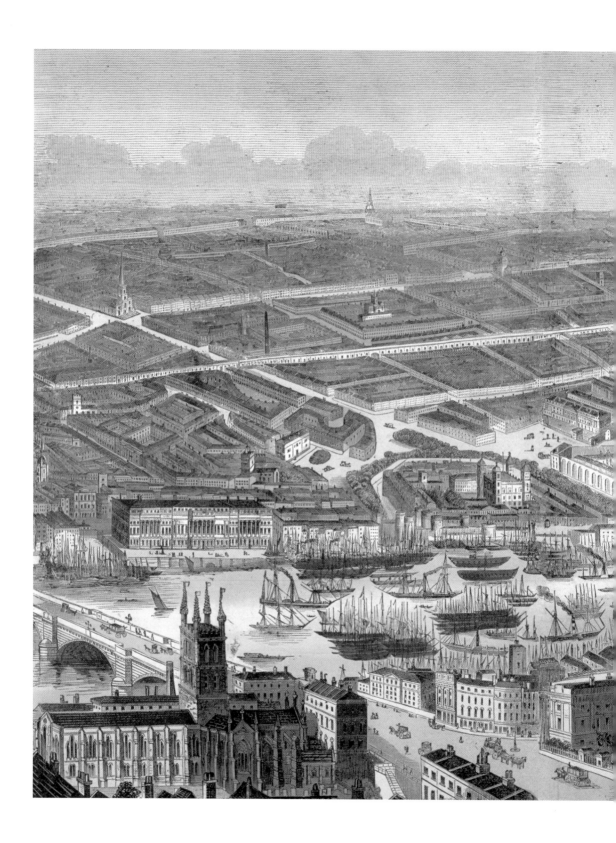

View of East London, 1850

*In the nineteenth century, the
area to the east of the Tower of
London and Aldgate pump was
transformed by the building of
the London Docks (1805) and
then St Katharine's Dock (1828).
A new road, the Commercial
Road (1802–30), linked the City
of London to the East and West
India Docks at Blackwall and
Poplar. By the time that this print
was made, the London and
Blackwall Railway (1840) had
been built and ran on a raised
viaduct through East London.*

CREATION OF A MYTHOLOGY

Thus far we have examined the origins of a range of social concerns about the condition of east London. For the most part they lacked coherence because the connections between, say, poverty and disease were so little understood. In the course of the nineteenth century, however, these various discourses were brought together to form a powerful myth that framed perceptions of its diverse districts. The process was complex, and here we can do no more than discuss briefly the principal participants.[8]

Henry Mayhew's flawed masterpiece *London Labour and the London Poor*, first published in 1851, begins with a discussion of costermongers. The condition of these street sellers, he claims, force us to

> contemplate the vast amount of vice, ignorance and want, existing these days in the very heart of our land. The public have but to read the following plain unvarnished account of the habits, amusements, dealings, education, politics, and religion of the London costermongers in the nineteenth century, and then to say whether they think it safe . . . to allow men, women, and children to continue in such a state.[9]

Costermongers of necessity congregate in the courts and alleys in the vicinity of the street markets, among the most important of which is Whitechapel. Here the poorer among them live in a state of near destitution, but one 'borne with so much content' simply because they had been spared from the workhouse. Many of these and other street sellers gravitate towards the low lodging-houses of Thrawl Street, Flower and Dean Street, Wentworth Street and Rosemary Lane where are found 'the worst places, both as regards filth and immorality'.[10] To emphasise the point Mayhew later includes an eyewitness account of conditions in a lodging-house in Brick Lane related by 'a man of superior education', which reveals an expansive range of social and moral concerns:

THE STREET-SELLER OF CROCKERY-WARE

BARTERING FOR OLD CLOTHES

Illustration of a street-seller from Henry Mayhew's London Labour and the London Poor, *1851.*

All the beds were occupied, single men being mixed with married couples. The question is never asked, when a man and woman go to a lodging house, if they are man and wife . . . The beds are average size. Dirt is the rule with them, and cleanliness the exception. They are all infested with vermin . . . There is no objection to any boy and girl occupying a bed, even though the keeper knows they were previously strangers to each other. The accommodation for the purposes of decency is very bad in some places . . . It is not uncommon for a boy or man to take a girl out of the streets to these apartments. Some are the same as common brothels, women being taken in at all hours of the day or night . . . They are the ready resort of thieves and all bad characters, and the keepers will hide them if they think they can from the police, or facilitate the criminal's escape . . . These houses are but receptacles for beggars, thieves, and prostitutes, and those *in training* for thieves and prostitutes.[11]

There are, however, Mayhew concludes, fewer such houses than in the past for some have been pulled down, others taken into improved management. This optimism was overstated, for the streets and houses he identified were to figure prominently in the heightened moral panic of the 1880s, in essence because the problem of housing, far from being resolved, actually deteriorated. Early in the century the landscape of east London was transformed by the construction of the vast modern docks complex. The completion of the West India Docks in 1802 was followed by Wapping, East India, Surrey and St Katharine's Docks, by which time London possessed the most extensive docks in the world. While the impact on local industries was slight, the construction

The building of St Katharine's Dock (detail), 1828, by W. Ranwell
Over 1,250 houses and tenements were demolished and 11,000 inhabitants displaced to make way for the new dock, alongside the Tower of London.

View of the West India Docks from the south east, *1840,*
by William Parrott

of the docks and new roads to facilitate communication forced clearance of large swathes of housing in the area of Whitechapel. When this was combined with the migration of thousands of labourers seeking work in the docks, the pressure on existing housing increased dramatically, leading to a steady deterioration in its condition.

From mid-century attention turned with renewed energy to improvement schemes as a means of facilitating communications and clearing slum areas. An increase in the population of Whitechapel had put pressure on housing at the lower end of the market, intensifying the presence of congested courts and alleys.

The call-on, London Dock, *c*.1889
Most dock work was casual. Each morning, just inside the dock gates, dockers were picked by the foreman. Many were turned away.

Ambitious street and slum clearance schemes were undertaken to eradicate these and similar districts in the metropolis, and so dissipate the anxieties about public health, crime and radicalism that they presented. The frenetic period of railway construction also impacted disproportionately on the poorest and most densely populated districts adjoining the City, including Bethnal Green and Whitechapel.[12] The hope that these various schemes would eradicate slum areas, however, proved futile, for what few at the time appreciated was that the tens of thousands of poor families displaced did not move out of the area, or into decent alternative accommodation since there was none, but simply migrated to nearby streets where slum conditions were recreated.

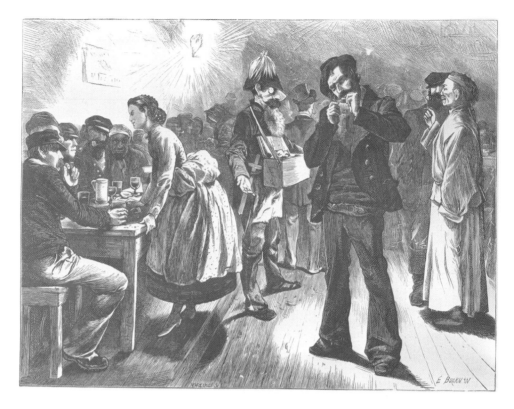

A sailors' assembly room at the East-End, *c.*1880
For a time, the police investigation into the Whitechapel murders focused on the docks and riverside wharves. The port district was close to Whitechapel and ships arrived regularly on particular days of the week. Various theories about the identity of the Whitechapel murderer focused on sailors, drovers and butchers working on cattle steamers.

By the 1880s the proportion of the population of Whitechapel living in overcrowded accommodation was exceeded only by that of the dockside area of St-George's-in-the East and Holborn, despite a net loss during 1851–81 of over 50,000 people due to migration from the district.[13]

The relationship between poverty and overcrowding, however, was not entirely clear. The great survey of Charles Booth which was undertaken in the 1880s, and first published as *Life and Labour of the People in London* in 1889, demonstrated that the most overcrowded districts were not necessarily the poorest, and that the poverty of east London compared to the rest of London had been consistently overstated. In a table ranking areas with more than 40 per cent poverty, Whitechapel appeared well below the slum areas of Southwark, Greenwich, Bermondsey and King's Cross. In comparison with St-George's-in-the-East, with 'a squalor peculiar to itself', Whitechapel possessed what for Booth was a certain attraction:

> The feeling that I have just described – this excitement of life which can accept murder as a dramatic incident, and drunkenness as the buffoonery of the stage – is especially characteristic of Whitechapel. And looked at this way, what a drama it is! Whitechapel is a veritable Tom Tiddler's ground, the eldorado of the East, a gathering together of poor fortune seekers; its streets are full of buying and selling, the poor living with the poor. Here just outside the old city walls, have always lived the Jews, and here they now are in their thousands, both old established and new comers, seeking their livelihood under conditions which seem to suit them on the middle ground between civilization and barbarism.[14]

It is apparent here that any sense of excitement was mitigated by a certain anxiety, for Booth, like so many contemporary observers, touched on the troubled question of immigration. From its beginnings east London had been a site of refuge for the dispossessed, persecuted and exiled. Many young migrants from all corners of the land found entry to the City barred, and so pursued opportunities provided by the growing industrial centres beyond the wall. Here too during the seventeenth and eighteenth centuries settled increasing numbers of Germans, Jews, Huguenots and in particular Irish. There was no shared experience, however; French Huguenots were generally welcomed since they soon proved their extraordinary skills as silk weavers,

Outcasts sleeping in sheds in Whitechapel, 1888
The Illustrated London News *sent one of its artists to the East End to illustrate the lonely courts and alleys where the murders had taken place. The magazine declared that such images 'must appeal to the humane feelings of regret and earnest desire to check the downward course of so many of our fellow-creatures in the foul places of great and mighty London'.*

providing employment and building fine houses, while Ashkenazi Jews from Poland and Germany, augmenting the Sephardic Jewish community that had settled from as early as the seventeenth century, established small workshops. The Irish, most of whom were unskilled labourers, gravitated towards employment in the docks, building and street trades where, as we have seen, they attracted much hostility because of their propensity to undercut the wages and hence employment of other sections.

As east London was subjected increasingly to the enquiring gaze of a variety of social commentators during the nineteenth century, so the separateness of immigrant communities was emphasised, most often by use of pejorative stereotypes. Watts Phillips in a book tellingly entitled *The Wild Tribes of London* (1855) sought to demonstrate how poor districts threatened the health and vitality of London. In a chapter devoted to Petticoat Lane, Whitechapel, he describes a 'Modern Babel . . . a perfect sea of greasy bargainers, blocking up the thoroughfare'. There is no other place in London that can compare with the filth of the lane; only in the Ghetto of Rome or the half Jewish cities of Hamburgh and Frankort (*sic*) can worse conditions be found. And if anyone believed that fences (receivers of stolen goods) were a dying breed, listen to the words of his 'official friend' from the neighbourhood: 'Spitalfields yonder, and Wentworth-street's close at hand – there are thieves all sides of us. They do the work, but who gets the pull? Why, the Jews. And where do you find 'em? Here, of course – here, about Petticoat Lane.'[15]

Working within the tradition of Mayhew, John Hollingshead published a series of letters under the rubric 'London Horrors' which subsequently appeared in the popular book *Ragged London in 1861*. In one of the letters he describes the condition of Whitechapel in ways that begin to state more explicitly the perceived links between dirt, poverty and racial degeneration. Claiming that Blackchapel might be a more appropriate name, he takes us to New Court located a few yards from Whitechapel High Street, wherein we are introduced to a

> nest of thieves, filled with thick-lipped, broad featured, rough-haired, ragged women, and hulking, leering men, who stand in knots, tossing for pennies, or lean against the walls at the entrances of the low courts. The houses present every conceivable aspect of filth and wretchedness . . . The faces that peer out of the narrow windows are yellow and repulsive; some are the faces of Jews, some of Irishwomen, and some of sickly-looking infants.[16]

This engraving was one of Gustave Doré's illustrations in the chapter 'Whitechapel and thereabouts' in London, a Pilgrimage *(1872). Douglas Jerrold's text spoke of 'forlorn men, women, and children — and a spacious township peopled with them, from cellars to attics — from the resort of the sewer rat to the nest of the sparrow in the chimney-stack — make up that realm of suffering and crime'.*

English colonies fare little better, except that there is a notable absence of racial coding. In George Yard, Wentworth Street and Castle Alley Hollingshead found that half the inhabitants were dock labourers, the other half being 'thieves, costermongers, and stall-keepers, professional beggars, rag-dealers, brokers and small tradesmen'.

It was from the 1860s that the East End poor were seen increasingly as a separate race threatening social order and the future of the Empire. Despite ambitious programmes of social and economic reform, the poor remained an atavistic presence at the very heart of London's commercial and symbolic might. Theories were launched that linked poverty to crime and hereditary degeneration, which if unchecked would spread contagion throughout the body of the nation.

Fate conspired to give considerable momentum to these pernicious deliberations. Following pogroms against the Jewish population in Eastern Europe during the 1880s tens of thousands of Ashkenazi Jews made their way to east London, augmenting dramatically a community that had successfully established itself around the Petticoat Lane market and in the clothing and cigar-making industries to the extent that they came to dominate the demographics of many local streets. They were not welcomed. In a typical article entitled 'Israel in London' published in 1900 in the *English Illustrated Magazine*, George Wade expressed disgust at the new immigrant community. Priding himself on knowledge of 'most of the foreign quarters of the East End', he stated that the 'most benighted of the Chinese and Hindu, to say nothing of the Irish and poorest English are simply paradise to the dirt and squalor of the Jewish district'.[17] This was the moment when figures such as Arnold White, fearing that such immigrant populations threatened the British Empire, began to campaign for restrictions on their entry.

During the troubled decade of the 1880s these profound social anxieties mounted because they quite suddenly assumed political significance. So long as the poor were confined to their dens in east London the immediate threat to metropolitan elites was slight, but then in a series of riots in 1886–87 the unemployed poor broke out of Whitechapel, Spitalfields, Stepney and West Ham to rampage across the West End, smashing shops and houses en route. Most worrying was the belief that the hordes were led and inspired by agitators who had been schooled in the dangerous doctrines of socialism; the prospect of the London poor organised and galvanised into action by the Social Democratic Federation struck terror in the heart of respectable opinion.[18]

1888

This was the backdrop against which the series of murders was committed in Whitechapel in the second half of 1888. Initially they attracted little attention for, as the local press reported, this was a time when violent crime in east London seemed on the increase. Late in August, before the first of the canonical murders, the conservative *East London Advertiser* expressed regret that in recent weeks it has had 'to chronicle an exceptional amount of crime which has been committed in the East End', but then proceeded to reassure its readers that

> there is no cause for despair over the state of the people. Strike an average in this generation and in the last, and when they are compared together, there will be shown a happy improvement in our condition. East London is now on a moral and social 'down grade', for the lower strata in our population, in which most of these evils arise, is slowly but surely being reached by the influences of a better age and a truer charity.[19]

Such reassurances were short lived, for within a week Polly Nichols' mutilated body was found in Buck's Row: the press, detecting a certain gruesome pattern, embarked on an extraordinary campaign of sensational reportage which lasted for three months and has served to frame endless speculation since. Typical was the radical daily evening newspaper the *Star*, which in its struggle to comprehend a frightening new phenomenon was forced to resort to comparison with fictionalised acts of the past:

> Nothing so appalling, so devilish, so inhuman – or, rather, human – as the three Whitechapel crimes has ever happened outside the pages of Poe or De Quincey. The unravelled mystery of 'The Whitechapel Murders' would make a page of detective romance as ghastly as 'The Murders in the Rue Morgue'. The hellish violence and malignity of the crime which we described yesterday resemble in almost every particular the two other deeds of darkness which preceded it. Rational motive there appears to be none. The murderer must be a Man Monster . . .[20]

For the *Evening Standard*, on the other hand, the murders were of much greater social significance. Refusing to take refuge in the idea of diabolical madness, it claimed that the events exposed the far more dangerous presence of latent savagery in 'degraded classes' located close to the very heart of London's commercial and imperial wealth. The 'monstrous and wanton brutality' of the crimes, it argued, is 'what we might expect of a race of savages than from even the most abandoned and most degraded classes in a civilised community'. The events were therefore symptomatic of the wholesale failure of the civilising tendencies of previous decades and a terrifying portent for the future:

> It is terrible to reflect that at the end of the nineteenth century, after all our efforts, religious, educational, and philanthropic, such revolting and sickening barbarity should still be found in the heart of this great City, and be able to lurk undetected in close contact with all that is most refined, elegant, and cultivated in human society.[21]

These imperial referents were highly significant, not least in revealing perceived connections between the metropolitan poor and colonial subjects in the far reaches of the British Empire. It was not long before commentators reminded readers that the events in Whitechapel were strikingly similar to the atrocities of the 1857 Indian revolt when British subjects were mutilated by foreign barbarians unrestrained by the precepts of Christian civilisation. As H. J. Tibbatts wrote to the editor of the *City Press*, 'Thirty years ago one used to read with a shudder of the barbarities practised during the Indian Mutiny upon defenceless women and children; but nothing can be much worse than what has happened here in Christian England.'[22] The *Pall Mall Gazette*, which under its editor, W. H. Stead, had gained a reputation for investigative journalism, went further in proposing that the Whitechapel murderer had reached new depths for he was 'as much a savage as an untamed Australian aborigine, yet utterly devoid of the courage which is the savage's sole redeeming virtue'.[23]

Given that a certain consensus seemed to exist on the un-English nature of the murderous activities, attention turned to the presence in east London of immigrant communities. The popular *Penny Illustrated Paper*, while attesting to the many 'healthy spots' and 'hopeful institutions' of the East End, found there 'squalid districts' which were the 'hunting grounds of some of the lowest and most degraded types of humanity to be found in any capital. It is there that the dregs of Continental cities deposit themselves.'[24] And the Reverend Tyler of Mile End New Town, in the course of an address to the Christian Instruction Association, stated that what London now had to fear was the 'importation of the scum and depraved characters from all parts of this and other countries . . . Dregs of society coming down, as they did, into London and occupying the low lodging houses, made the centre a very difficult one for the police to deal with.'[25] In the meantime, ugly rumours began to spread among a confused and frightened population that a Jew following an obscure blood right had sacrificed gentile prostitutes by cutting their throats.[26]

Seemingly more responsible commentators urged readers not to disregard the significance of the 'hideous condition in which thousands, tens of thousands, of our fellow creatures live in this boasted nineteenth century'. Underlying such legitimate social concern, however, was the same equation of the physical conditions of the urban landscape with the moral state of its inhabitants. At the heart of the 'most civilised' city in the world, opined the *East and West Ham Gazette*, there exist in cells hidden from 'the sight of day' children who are

> brought into the world only to become full of corruption, reared in terror, and
> trained in sin, till punishment and shame overtakes them too and thrusts them down
> to the black depth where their parents lie already lost and dead to all hope of moral
> recovery and social rescue.[27]

At the root of this profound social malaise were the squalid houses of 'pestering filth, crouching crime and moral plight' which bear testimony to the failures of society more generally to provide decent accommodation for poor Londoners. These failures created and perpetuated common lodging-houses which, unsurprisingly, provided ready and regular shelter for most of the victims. Following the inquest into the murder of Annie Chapman, the coroner drew attention to the fact that she lived principally in the common lodging-houses of Spitalfields, with the almost inevitable consequences:

> You who are constantly called to hear the sad tale of starvation, or semi-starvation,
> of misery, immorality, and wickedness which some of the occupants of the 6,000
> beds in this district have every week to relate at coroner's inquests, do not require to
> be reminded of what life in a Spitalfields lodging house means.[28]

Towards the end of September 1888 fears reached a new pitch. The extraordinary Tenniel cartoon *Nemesis of Neglect* appeared in *Punch*, accompanied by a long poem on the Stygian darkness of east London. On the very next day the double murder was discovered, provoking another wave of press hysteria. The *Star* speculated that this

THE NEMESIS OF NEGLECT.

"THERE FLOATS A PHANTOM ON THE SLUM'S FOUL AIR,
  SHAPING, TO EYES WHICH HAVE THE GIFT OF SEEING,
INTO THE SPECTRE OF THAT LOATHLY LAIR
    FACE IT—FOR VAIN IS FLEEING!
RED-HANDED, RUTHLESS, FURTIVE, UNERECT,
'TIS MURDEROUS CRIME—THE NEMESIS OF NEGLECT!"

This famous image by John Tenniel for Punch *depicts Jack the Ripper as a phantom brandishing a knife and hovering over the Whitechapel slums.*

was the work of 'fiendish revenge for fancied wrongs, or the deed of some modern Thug or Sicarius',[29] but then gave a stark warning of a failure to heed the plight of the East End:

> Above all, let us impress the moral of this awful business on the consciences and the fears of the West-end. The cry of the East-end is for light – the electric light to flash in the dark corners of its streets and alleys, the magic light of sympathy and hope to flash into the dark corners of wrecked and marred lives. Unless these and other things come, Whitechapel will smash the Empire, and the best thing that can happen to us is for some purified Republic of the West to step in and look after the fragments.

Using identical rhetoric – but different historical referents – the Reverend W. E. Kendall of Bow sermonised on the 'Moral and Social Aspects of the Murders', and ended with a warning of the dire consequences of inaction:

> Next year Paris celebrates the centenary of her great revolution. He feared the French people are more than one hundred years ahead of us in revolutionary experience. Unless something was done and done soon, for the destitute masses of London and other cities of this Empire, we should have not a centenary of revolution, but a revolution itself.[30]

These contemporary observations help shed light on the complex ways in which Whitechapel was constructed as a site of disgust, danger and moral desolation. Much of the language had been evident in earlier periods when the district had been identified as a source of concern, but the events of 1888 served to focus and hence greatly intensify respectable Victorian opinion by bringing together into a fearful whole the various strands of social, moral and political rhetoric. This is the real historical significance of the Whitechapel murders, and the real legacy was their role in helping to create a myth that remains to this day.

To end on a note of caution: powerful though this myth has been, it has never gone unchallenged. Even at the height of the panic created by the press and various contemporary observers, there were many quieter voices that spoke of a different East End. The well-known journalist George Sims in an article on Stepney recalled that inhabitants of a locality are always

> jealous, and properly jealous, of their local fair name. Whitechapel rose as one man to protest against the atrocities of the Ripper being headlined in the press, 'The Whitechapel Murders'. The indignant Whitechapel folk explained, with much emotion, that the murders were committed in Spitalfields.[31]

And in a letter to *The Times*, the Reverend Samuel Barnett, long-time resident of Whitechapel, vicar of St Jude's, founder of Toynbee Hall and much else besides, reminded the public that criminal haunts forming the backdrop to the murders were of limited extent. 'The greater part of Whitechapel is as orderly as any part of London,' he explained, 'and the life of most of its inhabitants is more moral than that of many whose vices are hidden by greater wealth.'[32] His wife, Henrietta, commenting on the letter, testified to the virtues of the sort of 'abandoned women' who had become victims: 'only those who know them personally and intimately, as I did by the hundred, can know the readiness to help, the capacity for sacrifice, the generosity of heart, and the disregard of self that survives all the horrors of their lives.'[33]

No accounts written by a poor inhabitant of the area exist for here was a population sustained by oral not literary traditions, but this alternative sense of the East End is echoed time and again in comments of observers who could claim with some legitimacy to know its people. An account of 1885, written by a 'night nomad' with an introduction by Arnold White putatively confirming its authenticity, tells of the truly surprising cheerfulness and bonhomie that exists amid the misery of the lives of east Londoners. A man will give away his last copper and walk the streets to help pay

Old clothes sellers, Chrisp Street, Poplar, *c.*1905
Countering the commonly held view that the East End was a depressing
and gloomy place, this image shows a group of smiling and laughing women.
One can almost hear their lively market banter.

A Whitechapel street, *c.*1905
Pedestrians walk in the street past market stalls and shops. Suits and coats hung
on rods extend over the pavement into the roadway.

'for another's doss' when the recipient has been without a bed for successive nights.[34] E. Dixon, writing on 'A Whitechapel Street', claimed that he enjoyed living in the area because the 'very heterogeneous democracy of the East is infinitely more interesting than the *blasé* aristocracy of the West . . . There is an almost inexhaustible fund of interest in Whitechapel to him who has eyes to see, ears to hear, nostrils not too fastidious, and some sort of sensibility to be touched.'[35]

In July 1901 an article entitled 'The worst street in London' appeared in the *Daily*

Mail. It purported to describe the state of Dorset Street, Spitalfields, the 'head centre' of the shifting criminal population of London. This is, the author concluded, because of the persistence of lodging-houses, wherein we find 'depths below the lowest deep'.[36] The article met with a furious response from the inhabitants of Dorset Street and its neighbourhood. A hastily convened meeting had to be postponed because the pub room booked could not take the crowd that had gathered, and so a larger hall was booked for five days later. Even that proved too small and many could not gain entry. Present were many local employers and priests, but the bulk of the audience comprised poor inhabitants. Together they listened to Jack McCarthy who in a speech of nearly two hours denounced allegations made in the article:

> Dorset Street, Spitalfields, has sprung into undesired notoriety; here we have a place
> which boasts of an attempt at murder once a month (a voice said, why, he ought to
> be smothered) (Lies, wicked lies) and one house a murder in every room (what lies
> he tells, surely he is the champion at telling 'em), as a rule, policemen go down in
> pairs, hunger walks prowling in its alleyways, and the criminals of tomorrow are
> being bred there today (cries of lies, lies, where does he get his information from).
> Now gentlemen, is there *an attempt*? At murder once a month? (no, no, that there
> a'nt, does he take us for cannibals?).

These sentiments were echoed briefly by other local inhabitants who declared that the article was false from start to finish, a gross libel on a body of working people.

It was rare, however, for such views of east London to enter the realm of print. They clearly did not provoke the same level of righteous indignation and fear among the reading public, nor did they guarantee increased sales of newspapers, but they do need to be considered in any assessment of the imaginative landscape of Whitechapel, or indeed any other part of east London in the nineteenth century.

Petticoat Lane, *c.*1900

The largest and oldest street market in the East End drew tens of thousands of Londoners on a Sunday morning. Situated on the eastern border of the City of London, it had been renamed Middlesex Street in the early Victorian period, even though the market continued to be called Petticoat Lane in common parlance. Nearby Wentworth Street was known generally to locals as just 'the Lane' where the market operated during the week.

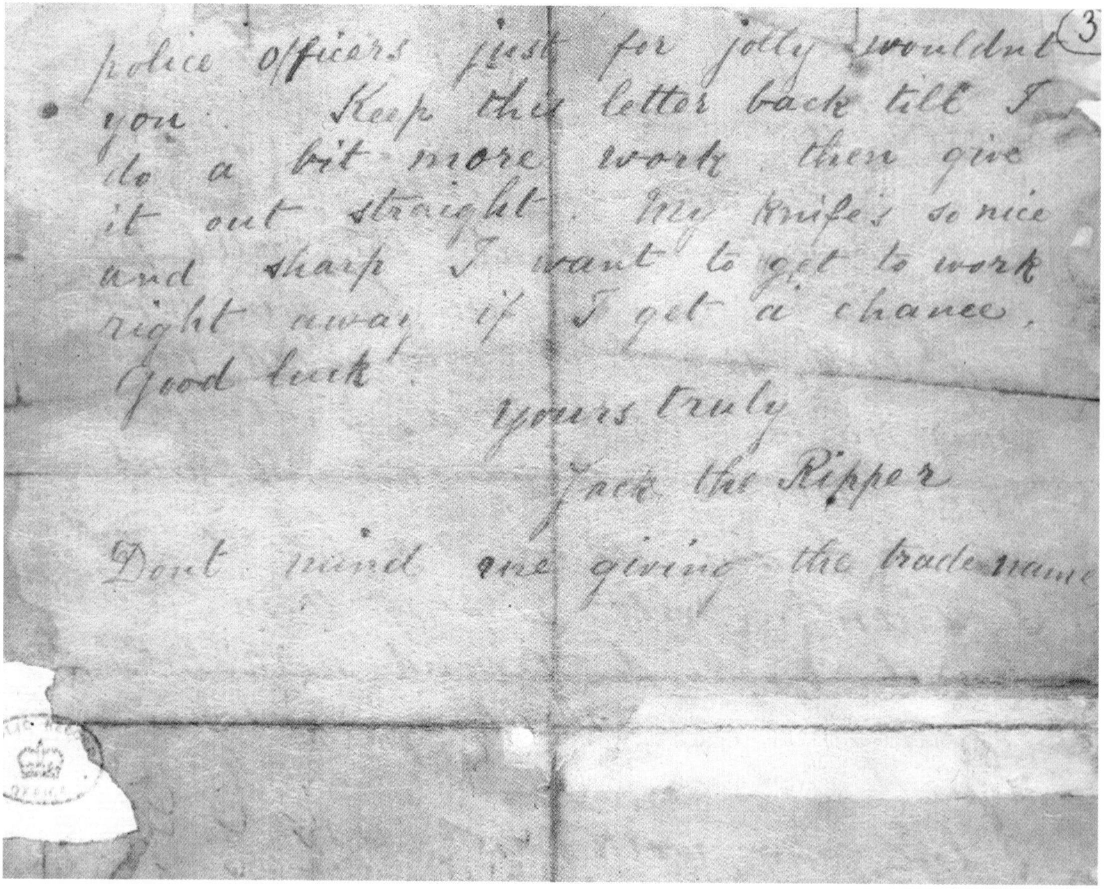

police officers just for jolly wouldn't
you. Keep this letter back till I
do a bit more work then give
it out straight. My knife's so nice
and sharp I want to get to work
right away if I get a chance.
Good luck.

yours truly

Jack the Ripper

Dont mind me giving the trade name

PLATE 1. *Richard Mansfield, the actor, as Dr Jekyll and Mr Hyde, c.1888. Just a few nights after the play opened at the Lyceum, Martha Tabram was brutally murdered in Whitechapel. Some felt that the performance had inspired the savagery of the killer.*

PLATE 2. *Detail of* Dear Boss *letter, 25 September 1888*
The letter was received three days before the night of the double murder of Elizabeth Stride and Catherine Eddowes. This makes the supposed killer's taunting words all the more chilling.

PLATE 3. *Detail from Charles Booth's* Descriptive Map of London Poverty, *1889, showing the location of the Whitechapel murders. With the murders taking place with such regularity and in such close proximity, the police began to refer to each new incident as 'another Whitechapel'.*

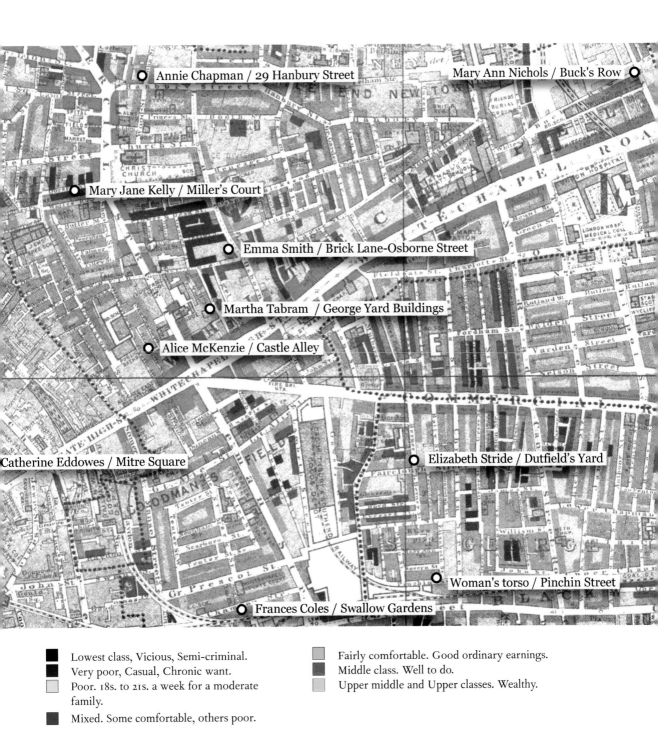

Annie Chapman / 29 Hanbury Street

Mary Ann Nichols / Buck's Row

Mary Jane Kelly / Miller's Court

Emma Smith / Brick Lane-Osborne Street

Martha Tabram / George Yard Buildings

Alice McKenzie / Castle Alley

Catherine Eddowes / Mitre Square

Elizabeth Stride / Dutfield's Yard

Woman's torso / Pinchin Street

Frances Coles / Swallow Gardens

Lowest class, Vicious, Semi-criminal.
Very poor, Casual, Chronic want.
Poor. 18s. to 21s. a week for a moderate family.
Mixed. Some comfortable, others poor.

Fairly comfortable. Good ordinary earnings.
Middle class. Well to do.
Upper middle and Upper classes. Wealthy.

Plan of Mitre Square and surroundings

Scene of Murder . 1·45· A.M. Sunday Sep.r 30.th 1888 .

— Scale of feet —

FOR FURTHER DETAILS SEE PLAN 2.

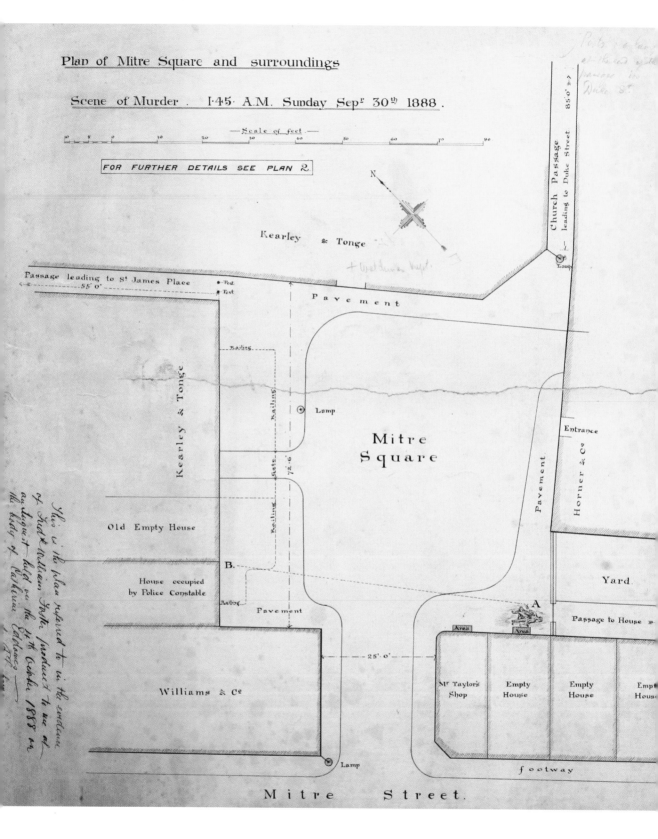

Kearley & Tonge

N

Church Passage leading to Duke Street

85'0"

Passage leading to St James Place

55' 0"

Post
Post

Pavement

Lamp

Railing

Railing

Gate

72'·6'

Kearley & Tonge

Lamp

Mitre Square

Entrance

Horner & Co

Pavement

Old Empty House

B.

House occupied by Police Constable

Railing

Yard

Pavement

A

Area   Area

Passage to House

25' 0"

Williams & Co

M.r Taylor's Shop

Empty House

Empty House

Empt House

Lamp

footway

Mitre Street.

This is the plan referred to in the evidence of Fred. William Foster, Surveyor to the city at inquest held on the 4th October 1888 on the body of Catharine Eddowes
Fred. W.m Foster

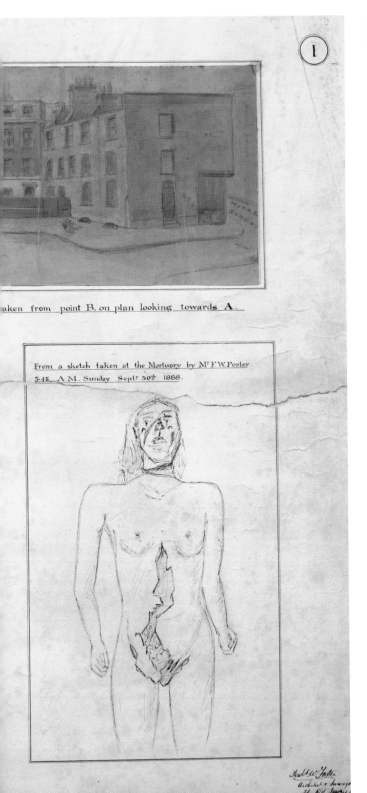

aken from point B. on plan looking towards **A.**

From a sketch taken at the Mortuary by Mr F. W. Foster
5·45. A.M. Sunday Septr 30th 1888.

PLATES 4, 5, 6. *Frederick W. Foster,
son of the superintendent of the City of
London Police, produced this scaled plan
at the inquest into the death of Catherine
Eddowes. Two drawings by Dr Frederick
Gordon Brown, the City Police's surgeon,
recorded the position of the body and
detail of the mutilations.*

PLATE 7. *John Henry Henshall's* Behind the Bar, *a watercolour of 1882, shows the dangers of alcohol. The viewer glimpses the regular patrons of the pub including a mother feeding her baby gin and the faces of the inebriated. A pawnbroker's shop hints at the hard times to follow for those succumbing to drink.*

☞ PLATE 8. *Whitechapel, detail from Charles Booth's original hand-coloured Map of Poverty, c.1888–9. It differs in colouring from the published version (1889) and contains clearer information about individual streets.*

'No Englishman could have perpetrated such a horrible crime . . . It must have been done by a Jew'

THE IMMIGRANT COMMUNITY OF WHITECHAPEL AT THE TIME OF THE RIPPER MURDERS

ANNE J. KERSHEN

Following the discovery of the body of Annie Chapman, the *East London Observer* of 15 September 1888 reported on the increase of anti-alienism[1] in the district of Whitechapel and the 'threatening attitude towards the Hebrew population of the district'. In many ways it is not surprising that crimes of such an alien nature should be blamed upon an alien community. The shock and revulsion at these serial sexual murders encouraged people to look beyond national borders for a scapegoat; and what better scapegoat than the outsider, the foreigner. If the finger were to be pointed, then where else but at the Eastern European Jewish community whose visible concentration in and around the area in which the Ripper's victims had been found made it an obvious target. This is not to say that there were no other *foreigners* in the district, but while these, with the exception of the small German community which numbered some 5,000, could be counted in tens and twenties, the aliens – as the local foreign Jewish community was known – totalled between 80,000 and 100,000.[2]

There had been a Jewish presence at the eastern edge of the City of London since 1656. In that year, 366 after their expulsion from England, Oliver Cromwell agreed to the readmission of Jews and the overt practice of Judaism in England. Initially the number of settlers was small. Even so, by the beginning of the eighteenth century, having established synagogues and acquired burial grounds, an east London Jewish community clearly existed.[3] Jewish immigration continued during the eighteenth century, and by the 1760s those emanating from Central and Eastern Europe significantly outnumbered their Sephardi co-religionists. There was a respite in migration during the French wars but the movement began again in the late 1830s, and by the 1870s the initial trickle was becoming a flood. By the time of the Ripper murders the settlement of Jews in the East End was conservatively estimated to be in the region of 70,000 to 80,000 though a realistic figure would be between 100,000 and 120,000. The majority were packed tightly into the traditional place of first settlement for immigrants, Spitalfields, an area of some 200 acres bounded to the west by Bishopsgate/North Folgate/Middlesex Street; to the north by Shoreditch/Bethnal Green/Quaker Street/Buxton Street through to Vallance Road; to the east, southwards down Brady Street to Whitechapel Road, the latter forming the district's southern boundary. As numbers increased the community spilled over south of Whitechapel Road, though not beyond the Highway, and east towards Mile End. To Jews living in overcrowded and insanitary conditions, with employment largely casual and seasonal, the promised land must have seemed a long way away.

As part of the massive westward migration of the late nineteenth century, Jews from Russia and Russia-Poland were seeking a promised land which offered financial opportunity in an environment of religious and political freedom. The accelerated movement was not, as some have suggested, predominantly because of the terror of

At the docks: arrival by a German steamer, 1903.
From Living London, *edited by George R. Sims.*
It was often steamers from Hamburg that transported Jewish immigrants to London.
The ships moored in midstream near the London and St Katharine's Docks and the
passengers were rowed ashore in small boats to one of the riverside stairs.

the pogroms. In reality the Eastern European Jews were escaping hunger, reduced economic opportunity and, for many, unemployment. They left behind them poverty and hopelessness, and brought with them memories of a life which can only have existed when seen through the lens of rose-tinted glasses. As a means of understanding what the experience of migration and settlement was for those late nineteenth-century arrivals we need first to explore what life was like in the *shtetls* of the Pale of Settlement.

THE *SHTETL*

The *shtetl* defied geographic parameters or specific locations and has been defined as 'any settlement inhabited by Jews'. It was a myth created by those who lived in it, packaged, taken overseas and passed on to future generations. As one migrant explained, 'My home is the family and the family activities, not the walls or the yard or the broken-down fence.' The *shtetl* was not simply a dot on a map, it was a state of mind which incorporated the rural and the urban. It was the stronghold of Ashkenazic culture, where Jews spoke Yiddish, wrote and read Hebrew, and bargained in broken Polish and Ukrainian. It was the essence of the construct transported by migrants to the modern cities of the Pale of Settlement[4] – such as Odessa, Warsaw and Lodz – and overseas to New York's lower east side and the East End of London. In the *shtetl* Jews were never isolated from the non-Jewish population, even when in the majority there was a frequent influx of Christians from outside for markets and fairs and, though the language of the Pale was Yiddish, there were those Jews who spoke Russian and Polish, plus other native tongues. In this way, some – though not all – of the emigrants were prepared for the interactive life they would find in their future places of settlement.

The architecture of religion dominated the *shtetl*. Churches and synagogues of imposing size and design, their black wood exteriors hiding a riot of colour on the inside, commanded and demanded of their congregants. Other public buildings included religious bathhouses (*mikvahs*) and *cheders* (religious schools) – secular schools were a late arrival on the Russian education scene, where standards were poor for both Jew and gentile. Most *shtetl* 'houses' consisted of one or perhaps two rooms, with plastered and whitewashed interiors, and floors which were at best made of boards, more often of earth. Bed-sharing was the rule, children sharing with siblings and often with mother as well, father occupying a sofa; sleeping and eating quarters

This photograph shows a Russian boarding house used by Jewish immigrants
on their journey to London and New York, 1891

were separated by a curtain. The myth of home carefully censored the reality of filthy, uncobbled streets paved with upturned wooden boxes which served as stepping-stones, and which were covered with dirty snow in winter and swamped in spring. In summer, pedestrians had to manoeuvre around. As one immigrant described it,

> the dust piles in thick layers which the rain changes to mud so deep that wagon wheels stick fast and must be pried loose by the sweating driver . . . After rain, streams and puddles of muddy water . . . when the mud gets too bad, boards are put down over the black slush so that people can cross the street.

By comparison Whitechapel Road and Brick Lane must have seemed, if not the promised land, then certainly the gateway to it.

In the Pale of Settlement, Jews were active on most levels of the economy, the majority, approximately 74.3 per cent, engaged in unskilled, artisanal and petty trades, a further 3.5 per cent working in agriculture. Not surprisingly in a culture which revered learning and study, the unskilled and semi-skilled earned little respect. Unlearned men lacked 'prestige, respect, authority and status . . . it was they who thronged the market place'. To be a tailor was to be stigmatised and for many forced to turn to the production of clothing, it was a condition 'which brought shame [to] my family'. In contrast, poverty on the part of a prospective bridegroom was unimportant if the future son-in-law was a budding rabbi. As the nineteenth century progressed, Jewish economic life became one of low wages, interspersed with long periods of unemployment in an environment of increasing hopelessness. Urbanisation created a large semi-skilled and unskilled proletariat, which was poverty stricken, diseased and slum ridden, 90 per cent living from hand to mouth. Writing about urban life in Belorussia in 1875, the founding father of Jewish social-ism, Aaron Liberman, recorded that Jewish workers lived in 'the semi-darkness of cellars and similar hovels that had wet under floors . . . crammed together in an oppressive stupefying atmosphere'. The Jewish population was ground down even further by the Russian government's policy of extracting as much money as possible through the imposition of a system of local and national dual taxation.

It was the ever-increasing impoverished and hopeless urban proletariat that provided the source of migrants. Emigration was increasingly perceived as a solution to the ongoing hardships and, in spite of the bureaucratic and financial difficulties of migration, the young men (and women) of the Pale of Settlement emigrated. The opportunities offered by the 'golden' cities of London and New York were well known, descriptions – doubtless embellished by the time they reached the furthest outposts of the Pale of Settlement – acting as magnets for those who saw in *shtetl* life only despair and misery. They travelled westwards to find a new and better life, if not for themselves then for their children and grandchildren. Not all found the *golde medinhe* (golden land) and not all stayed. In spite of the myths of Jewish success, in the early years of immigrant settlement there were those, some 50,000, who returned to Eastern Europe, having found London too hard and too cruel. By doing this they were not fulfilling the accepted 'myth of return'; rather, they had been let down by the myth of elsewhere. For the reality was that, in the early years of Eastern European settlement and assimilation, only the ruthless few made it out of the East End Jewish ghetto.

A PROMISED LAND?

The prerequisite for newly arrived immigrants in any location is a place to live and work. The ambitions of the Eastern European immigrants were no different. Some were joining kin or *landsleit* (people from the same town or village) who could provide them with initial accommodation and jobs. Others had to fend for themselves. For those with nowhere to go, a maximum of two weeks' temporary accommodation was available at the Poor Jews Temporary Shelter in Leman Street, south of Whitechapel Road on the periphery of the Jewish East End. The shelter, used predominantly by transmigrants en route to North America and South Africa, was established in 1885 by a group of Jewish philanthropists who recognised the need to care for their co-religionists and prevent their making demands on the public purse via institutions such as the workhouse. In addition to the economic dimension was the concern that indigent Jews be able to maintain the tenets of their religion. By the middle of the nineteenth century, a network of Jewish charities was in place in London which covered 'the needy, the hungry, the mad, the orphaned, the blind and the sick, not to mention the rituals of life from birth to burial'. Spitalfields boasted a Jewish Ladies' Association for Preventive and Rescue Work, an organisation set up to save single, female migrants from the white slave trade; a Soup Kitchen for the Jewish Poor (in Fashion Street); a Jewish Working Men's Club and five *mikvahs*. This

Russian refugees in the Poor Jews Temporary Shelter, Leman Street, 1891
An engraving by Ellen Gertrude Cohen.

blanket coverage was fully in keeping with the Jewish religious doctrine of *tzedekah* (charity) laid down by the rabbis centuries before.

The programme of road, railway, dock and canal development that was part of the capital's response to the demands of nineteenth-century industry and empire had a largely negative effect on the population of the East End. As the labyrinthine alleyways and rookeries that had provided sanctuary for those escaping the long arm of the law were demolished, homes disappeared and, with no state or local government

72

rebuilding policy,[5] housing conditions for pauper immigrant and indigene alike were, in simple terms, overcrowded, over-priced and insanitary. Newly arrived 'greeners' and casual workers were forced to rely on Jewish charities or on the mercies of the unscrupulous Jewish landlords of Spitalfields. The rent for a single room could be anything from 4 to 7 shillings a week, figures which could represent between 25 and 30 per cent of a tailor's income (when he was in work). In return for this the tailor and his family would be provided with accommodation that was invariably cramped and dirty. Yet the alien immigrant was determined in spirit, if not always successful in body, and prepared to pay the higher rents, endure subletting and pay key money, if that was what it took to live and work in 'Little Jerusalem', the name given to the district which had become the Jewish quarter, and which was perceived as the starting-point of upward mobility for the incomer.

In spite of its epithet, particularly in the 1860s and 1870s the area was not exclusively Jewish. The Decennial Census shows that Eastern European cap-makers and Irish shoemakers occupied the same tenement houses, living one floor above the other. In this way, irrespective of linguistic and religious differences, points of social – and possible economic – interaction developed. This immigrant interface continued in the decades ahead, the Decennial Census for 1891 and the survey carried out for Charles Booth at the close of the nineteenth century illustrating that, although some streets might be 'all Jewish', others retained their social and ethnic mix. It was perhaps this interface that encouraged Irish dockers and Jewish tailors to provide political and financial support for each other during the dock and tailoring strikes of 1889 and 1912. However, the best-remembered and most dramatic example of support came during the now mythologised Battle of Cable Street in 1936 when Irish dockers and Jewish workers stood shoulder to shoulder against the police to ensure that Oswald Mosley's Blackshirts 'did not pass'.

By the 1870s the colony of Dutch and Polish Jews, many housed in and around what was ironically called Fashion Street, was expanding in all directions as fresh waves of immigrants from Russia and Russia-Poland arrived. Anglo-Jewry, having achieved full emancipation only in 1871, was becoming increasingly concerned by the reaction of the receiving society to the seemingly never-ending influx of their Eastern European co-religionists. On the domestic front, Jews were being criticised for their unhygienic domestic habits and their 'horrible smells'. The *East London Observer* – never the best friend of the alien Jew – reported on the appalling state of the immigrants' homes:

> Foreign Jews . . . either do not know how to use the latrine, water and other sanitary accommodation provided, or prefer their own semi-barbarous habits and use the floor of their rooms and passages to deposit their filth. Even in places where caretakers see that yards and closets are cleared away every morning, dirt and destruction follow the same day.

Although the description was somewhat hyperbolic, the elite of British Jewry lost no time in reacting. In 1885 it set up an East End Enquiry Commission under the chairmanship of Lord Rothschild. In its first report the Commission confirmed that many of the houses occupied by the 'Jewish poor' were either 'barely fit or utterly unfit' for human habitation. It recommended that 'steps must be taken to cause the foreign poor upon arrival to imbibe notions proper to civilised life in this country' and to improve the immigrants' physical surroundings. The recommendations were a clear pronouncement of the 'ironing out of the ghetto bends' strategy of Anglo-Jewry, additionally manifest in moves such as the establishment of the Jewish Lads' Brigade in 1895 and the banning of the use of Yiddish at the Jews' Free School.[6]

☞ *This lantern slide shows the inner yard area of the Charlotte de Rothschild Dwellings in Flower and Dean Street where residents hung their washing out to dry.*

The tangible outcome of the Commission's report was the construction of Rothschild Buildings in Flower and Dean Street, Spitalfields. In place of the labyrinth of rookeries emerged a model dwelling, named after Lord Rothschild's mother Charlotte. Accommodating artisans – the poorer inhabitants of the district could not support the cost or regularity of rent payments – 'the buildings' became home to a predominantly, though not completely, Jewish tenancy. What the new tenants could not have known when they moved in was that almost eighteen months later they would be living in the area that was to be the focus of the 'Jack the Ripper' murders and which as a result would become, in the 1890s, a redevelopment site. In place of the small, mean houses and rookeries in Flower and Dean Street, Thrall Street and those contiguous, emerged Nathaniel Buildings, Charlotte de Rothschild Buildings, Lolesworth Buildings, Irene House and Ruth House. The area took on a veneer of respectability, the loafers, semi-criminals and prostitutes such as Ripper victims Annie Chapman and Polly Nichols, having been confined to the few squalid lodging-houses that remained on the edges of Flower and Dean Street and Brick Lane.

In spite of the rebuilding that took place following the revelations that accompanied the Ripper murders, the image of Spitalfields as an overcrowded, unhealthy and exotic ghetto persisted. In the early twentieth century there were still people living in properties with no running water and, in the Jewish-owned Booth Street Buildings, there were just thirty water closets for 600 people. Some twelve years after the Ripper murders, the American journalist and author Jack London recorded his journey into the abyss that was the East End. He described the colour and texture of life in Spitalfields as 'grey and drab . . . the people themselves are filthy . . . the rain when it falls is more like grease than water from heaven'. In his revelatory book, *The People of the Abyss* (1903), London portrayed the East End as analogous to the darkest jungles of Africa. He described the appalling conditions he encountered in a seven-roomed house in Frying Pan Alley, just off Brick Lane. Six of the rooms (rented out at the going rate or more) measured no more than 8 ft by 8 ft. In these were housed 20 people who cooked, ate, slept and worked in the same space. In the seventh room, measuring 7 ft by 8 ft, he found five sweated (male) workers making shoes.

Writing at the same time Charles Russell and Harry Lewis recorded that:

> The two-storied tenement . . . having been often displaced by the model dwellings, which shelter hundreds of families upon a comparatively narrow site . . . [the Jew] overcrowds his home, and therefore can afford to pay a higher price than that previously obtained and therefore gradually displaces the gentile population.

At the weekend alien life overflowed on to the surrounding streets. Sydney Gelberg portrayed Middlesex Street (best known as Petticoat Lane) and its environs on a Sunday as a 'howling living pandemonium of cosmopolitan costerism, a curious tangle of humanity'. A walk along the same route more than a hundred years later reveals that, while the majority ethnic population may have changed in origin, the ambience of the area remains. Gelberg painted a picture of contrasts; of impoverishment and survival, hardship and vibrancy. If the weekends were a colourful tapestry then,

> On the weekday however the scene is transformed . . . you are in a city of endless toil . . . All day long, and far into the night, the factories make dismal music in the ghetto . . . Why do the Jews labour so? . . . [they are] alien Dick Whittingtons inside curls and *jupizes* (long coats) who have put down their bundles a while to peer into the promised land beyond and thereafter rest not till they have retired beaten from the struggle or found social salvation in Maida Vale . . . And if the ghetto is not wholly poor it is not entirely famished. Kosher restaurants abound in it; kosher butcher shops are clustered in their bunches . . . Altogether, indeed, a unique little cosmos, this East End

Hebrew colony – a poverty stricken, wealthy, hungry, feasting, praying, bargaining fragment of a 'Nation of Priests'.

Gelberg was right in his assertion that praying and feasting were two pillars of the East End, indeed any, Jewish community. As the immigrant community grew in size so did the number of places of prayer which accommodated the requirements of the incomers. The new arrivals of the second half of the nineteenth century had little empathy with the cathedral synagogues of the Anglo-Jewish establishment. The Great, the Hambro and the New, in 1870 united under the title United Synagogue, were perceived as tools of Anglicisation, reflecting little of the warmth and vitality that, for the Eastern European Jewish male, made his synagogue so much more than just a place of worship. In place of the cold, expansive, impressive and decorous edifices, the immigrants worshipped in the small *chevrots* (small synagogues) which blossomed all over the East End and could be found in back extensions to Huguenot houses, as in Princes Street, in converted or operative workshops in Hanbury and Fashion Street, or in what had once been Calvinist churches, as was Sandys Row Synagogue which opened in 1870. In strict contrast to their Anglicised co-religionists the Eastern European worshipped with a degree of indecorous self-abandonment, rejoicing in the traditional tunes that formed part of the service and, at times, breaking off from prayer to discuss the low piece rates in the tailoring trade, or problems of life in the Pale as reported by a new arrival from *der heim*. The author Israel Zangwill captured the passion and alien nature of the style of worship in *Children of the Ghetto*, his novel which portrayed all the pain and pleasure of life in the Jewish East End:

> The method of praying at these things was equally complex and uncouth . . .
> here a rising and there a bow, now three steps backwards and now a beating of
> the breast, this bit for the congregation and that for the minister; variations of
> a page, a word, a syllable, even a vowel, ready for every possible contingency.

St Mary's Church, Whitechapel, *c*.1900

John Galt's photograph shows the large Yiddish poster announcing a sermon at the church.

The *chevrot* was the male domain: women played no part in the service and when attending either sat at the back of the prayer hall, hidden from view behind a curtain or trellis, in a lofty women's gallery or, as Zangwill described it, in a room on a floor above through which the sound of the prayers could be heard, 'faintly through the flooring'.

For the immigrant in an alien land, the *chevrot* provided a bridge with home, the names resonant of the old country. Grodno Synagogue was located in Spital Street,

79

Kovno in Catherine Wheel Alley and the Warsaw Synagogue in Gun Street. The profusion of small places of worship that accompanied the expansion of the Jewish East End was viewed with concern by the Jewish establishment which considered the self-sufficiency and self-governance manifested by the *chevrots* and their members to be at odds with their desires for assimilation as rapidly as possible. These, allied to the insanitary nature of many of the places of prayer, galvanised the established Jewish community into action. Under the leadership of Samuel Montagu, Liberal MP for Whitechapel (later Lord Swaythling) a Federation of Synagogues was established in 1887; an initial sixteen synagogues were admitted, and others would be allowed entry when they were deemed suitable. In 1889 the Federation purchased a burial ground in north London. It would seem that in this way the Eastern European community had maintained religious autonomy. The reality was somewhat different, for with Lord Rothschild as President and Montagu as Vice- and Acting President the reins were very much in the hands of established Anglo-Jewry, which sought to bring the immigrants within the ambit of communal control.

Although the place of prayer played a central role in the life of the immigrant, acting additionally as club, friendly society, even employment exchange, this is not to imply that all Jews were regular attenders. Jewish employers were hard taskmasters and in the busy season many clothing workshop hands sweated late on Friday night and, when employers and finances demanded, even on the Sabbath. Others, young men delighting in the freedom they found away from the *shtetl*, directly flouted their religious roots and shocked the rest of the community by eating ham sandwiches outside the synagogue on the holiest of holy days, the Day of Atonement.

It is evident from the London street directories that in the 'Ripper Decade' the Jewish East End came into its own and the Eastern European Jewish community engraved its identity on the local landscape. In 1881 *Kelly's Post Office London Directory* street section lists just four Jewish-operated shops in Middlesex and Wentworth Streets;

Middlesex Street, looking south, with Stoney Lane on the right, *c.*1903
The large billboards, promoting the latest West End plays, were intended no doubt for the
thousands of Londoners who visited the popular Sunday market. At the time of the Whitechapel
murders, most of the shops along the street were Jewish owned. Trades included butchers,
ironmongers, hosiers, fried-fish shops, china and glass sellers, pickle dealers, greengrocers,
bootmakers, trimming sellers and even a 'passover cake manufacturer'.
In the photograph, probably taken on a relatively quiet Saturday 'Sabbath' morning,
most of the shops are boarded up and closed.

Levy Brothers Jewish bakery in Middlesex Street, Whitechapel, *c.*1900
Photograph by John Galt.

these included a butcher's and a grocer's. Eight years on, *Kelly's Post Office London Directory for 1889* provides us with a clear picture of the expansion of the community and its commercial heartland. In Brick Lane and the surrounding streets such as Fashion Street, Old Montague Street, Princes Street and Chicksand Street there was now a wealth of clothing workshops and Jewish retail outlets. The directory listed a baker (Aaron Levy), greengrocer (Samuel Levy) and butcher (Simon Zyschek), together with

The Original Kosher Wine Company in Osborn Street, *c.*1900
John Galt recorded the presence of Jewish businesses in the East End,
especially retailers of kosher food and drink.

several chandlers, and the occasional tobacconist. However, it was in west Spitalfields, in Wentworth Street and Middlesex Street, that Jewish food shopping took place.

One of the primary delights of the Jewish diet was the Sabbath eve chicken soup (called by some Jewish penicillin), a food which even the poorest housewife strove to provide. In order to conform with *halachah*[7] the fowl had to be supplied by a kosher butcher whose produce was approved by the religious board. By 1889, in Wentworth

A home workshop, *c.*1900
Whitechapel Mission lantern slide
A young man and woman can be seen making cigarettes by hand in a room which is
both workshop and bedroom. They are probably Jewish as a Tallit or Jewish prayer
shawl hangs from the clothes line.

and Middlesex Streets, there were no fewer than six kosher butchers' shops – one female owned. In addition there were two fishmongers and two fried-fish shops, one run by a Mrs Polly Nathan.[8] Evidence, surely, of the entrepreneurial activities of Jewish married women – though we do not know whether the lady butcher or Mrs Nathan were married or widowed.

Confirmation that the Jewish shops were restricted to the notional boundaries of the Jewish East End ghetto is provided by the fact that just beyond its border, in Aldgate High Street, though there were numerous meat salesmen and 'carcase' butchers, none of them bore a Jewish-sounding name. By 1894 Middlesex Street and Wentworth Street had become the hub of the local Jewish domestic economy. There were now eight butchers' shops, five grocers, two greengrocers, two pickle-makers, two bakers, one egg merchant, one provision dealer and Polly Nathan still selling fried fish. *The Jewish Year Book 1896* contains a list of butchers 'Licensed to sell Kosher Meat and Poultry for the year 1896': within the area embracing Aldgate eastwards to Mile End and Bethnal Green, and southwards to Commercial Road there are no fewer than 126 butchers and poulterers. This suggests not only the (increased) size of the community and their financial ability to purchase poultry, if not meat, but additionally the necessity for retail outlets to be close to the points of consumption. At the close of the nineteenth century, the Jewish East End was described by Litvinoff as a ghetto, 'Full of synagogues, backroom factories and little grocery stores reeking of pickled herring, garlic sausage and onion bread'.

It was a minority of the East End Jewish community that engaged in retail economic activity. The majority found employment in the seasonal, casual, semi-skilled sweated trades. Most of them worked in the tailoring trade – the Jewish association with which can be traced back to biblical times – but others toiled as cabinet-makers, slipper-makers, cap-makers and stick-makers. The coincidence of the improved earning capacity of artisans and white-collar workers, nearly all of whom thanks to British industry and Empire had sufficient surplus income to indulge in the purchase of new, rather than clobbered clothes, and the movement westwards of Russian-Polish Jewry, had facilitated the burgeoning of the wholesale clothing trade in the East End. In 1888, researching on behalf of her cousin Charles Booth, Beatrice Potter (later Webb) carried out a survey of tailoring workshops in the East End. Reportedly visiting them all, she found more than 900 in Whitechapel alone, located in cellars, attics and back rooms of domestic and commercial premises in the labyrinth of streets and alleyways that fed off the spine of Brick Lane.

Jewish tailor's workshop, 1891. *Engraving by Ellen Gertrude Cohen.*
Rooms in ordinary houses in Whitechapel and Spitalfields were converted into
small workshops. Here men, women and often children worked long hours in confined
and poorly ventilated workspaces.

In just one street there were thirty workshops, the majority producing jackets, the manufacture of which was the province of the male. Women were engaged in the lighter-weight side of the trade making vests (waistcoats) and trousers. Potter found that the majority of workshops were of small scale, employing under ten workers. Of the remainder she discovered 266 in which 10–20 hands were employed and 42 in which 25 people worked. Researching for the Board of Trade in 1887, John Burnett recorded several in which 50 hands were engaged in production, and even one of 100 workers. But for the most part, as economic history confirms, the belief prevailed that 'small was beautiful'.

Irrespective of size the tailoring workshops had a number of common factors. With few exceptions, conditions were barely tolerable. In 1883 one of Her Majesty's inspectors of factories unearthed a mantle and costume workshop in which nine hands worked in a room where the temperature never dropped below 86°F. In the busy season

Refugee on her way to join
her husband in America
Engraving, 1891.

work began before dawn and ended long after dusk. In the cellar workshops that abounded in Hanbury Street windows were either filthy or boarded up, with workers rarely seeing daylight for several days. Sanitary conditions were reportedly 'appalling'; internal water closets (where they existed) were filthy and often housed in cupboards adjacent to coal boilers. In addition to the obvious discomforts, the water closets constantly overflowed, while the workshop environment was hardly improved by the common practice of glazing poor-quality fabrics with urine.

Tailoring provided – erratic – employment for many of the immigrants, both skilled and unskilled, and in the closing decades of the nineteenth century there were

Middlesex Street, 1899

This image was taken by an amateur photographer who had an interest in London street life and immigrant districts. Jewish market traders and locals have stopped to pose for him.

few success stories. For although, as Beatrice Potter's research highlighted, a tailor could buy the status of employer with £1, the employer of one season became, with depressing regularity, the sweated employee of the next. Economic security and success were like water in the desert, and the immigrants from Eastern Europe the children of Moses: many glimpsed the future but few partook of the fruits. One of

Middlesex Street, 1903
In the left foreground, a stall holder can be seen laying out wet fish for sale.
On the right-hand side, the metal framework of a stall is being erected.

those who did turn the dream into reality was Morris Cohen, an immigrant who
arrived from Russia in 1877 with a 'slight knowledge of tailoring'. It did not take him
long to identify a gap in the London production system. An increasing number of
middle-class women were doing charitable work in working-class areas, taking tea in
ABC tea-shops and visiting department stores, playing outdoor sports such as golf

89

and hockey or participating in the craze for bicycling. He recognised that navy blue tweed and serge tailored jackets were far more suited to these activities and to rent-collecting in the East End and lecturing on the virtues of socialism and female suffrage than were the frills and flounces of the drawing rooms of Maida Vale and Mayfair. He was aware that there were no ladies' tailors in England; with the exception of women's riding habits, all the tailored fashion items were imported from Germany and France. Conscious of the opportunity for economic advancement, he took a selection of samples of women's tailored garments and persuaded a number of tailoring masters to make them up in their workshops. He then convinced wholesalers of the advantages of buying East End as opposed to overseas-made garments.

Within ten years Cohen employed 180 workers in his – and the country's – first custom-built mantle-making factory in Spital Square, Spitalfields. By the mid-1890s, his entrepreneurial activities were providing employment for 1,000 workers in ladies' tailoring all based in the East End. Cohen's achievement was acknowledged by the managing director of Hitchock Williams, a leading London wholesaler. In a letter to the *Jewish Chronicle* written in 1898, he praised the way Cohen had benefited British trade by significantly reducing the import of women's tailored garments – indeed the country was now exporting to Europe. He added further plaudit by stating that foreign Jews produced 'a class of work which our [English] workers cannot undertake with success'.

Achievements such as these were indeed rare but they did occur. Abraham R,[9] who engaged in 'financial dealing',[10] had moved west, out of Middlesex Street to Maida Vale, within twenty years of his arrival as an immigrant. Others such as Woolf Goldstein rose up the economic ladder by investing in property which he then let out at rack rents. But for the most part, life for the immigrants in the era of Jack the Ripper is best illustrated by this paragraph which appeared in the Yiddish radical newspaper, the *Arbeiter Fraint* (Worker's Friend):

It is heartbreaking to see how people, fathers of children, workers, good craftsmen work, so hard, such long hours with heads bent, tremble for their bosses, the majority caterers, shoemakers or drivers and all for what, for a slice of bitter bread in the busy time barely just to keep alive and, in the slack time so little . . .[11]

In spite of the hardship of immigrant life and the fact that, for the most part, rather than 'taking the jobs of Englishmen' as the myth would have it, the incomers developed their own particular branches of industry in response to contemporary economic and social trends, the reaction of the native society in the second half of the 1880s was negative. The aliens, pejoratively called by one trade unionist 'the refuse of the world', were condemned on both the domestic and the economic front. An article in the *Eastern Argus* which appeared in 1887, in the midst of over a decade of economic stagnation, illustrates both the attitude and the misconceptions. It read:

A number of men and women land on our wave-beaten shores in a destitute condition and offer to do work at any price . . . [this] drives English labour out of the labour market.

Another article, in the *East London Advertiser*, referred to the 'swarms of foreign Jews who have invaded the East End labour markets . . . [and] are chiefly responsible for the sweating system and the grave evils which are flowing from it'.

Others expressed concern at the perceived non-negotiable otherness of the immigrants and their children. The Reverend Reaney described the anger of those who

live and labour in the great East End [and] feel hot and angry at the sight of the faces so un-English and the sound of the speech so utterly foreign . . . In face, instinct, language and character their children are aliens, and still exiles. They seldom become citizens.

However, most vitriol was reserved for the domestic implications of the expand-ing and, by the closing years of the 1880s, highly visible alien community. Following on from an article which appeared in the *Lancet* in 1884 describing the appalling conditions in the alien sweatshops, the *East London Observer* recorded that

> Foreign Jews . . . either do not know how to use the latrine, water and other
> sanitary accommodation provided, or prefer their own semi-barbarous habits
> and use the floors of their rooms and passages to deposit their filth.

The writer seems to have overlooked the fact that the Medical Officer for Health in the district had repeatedly reported on the inefficiency of the water closets and the fact that, as a general rule, no more than 25 per cent were in working order. Charles Booth's volume on poverty, the first in the *Life and Labour of the People in London* series, which was published in 1889, did little to cool the flames. He summed up the situation in the following terms: 'No Gentile could live in the same house with these poor foreign Jews and even as neighbours they are unpleasant . . . The crowding that results is very great, and the dirt reported as indescribable.' Booth seems to have ignored the evidence of the census and his researchers which showed clearly that gentiles did live in the same houses as Jews, but then perhaps if the former were Irish it was not perceived as quite the same thing.

In addition to the issues which stemmed from a depressed economy and an overcrowded and inferior housing stock, there were tensions which had their roots in the perceived sexuality and criminality of migrants. It was believed that the alien Jew was involved with sex in the various roles of pimp, white-slave trader and prostitute. Sexual antagonism and envy are regular features of xenophobic vocabulary, and the castigations of Jews were, in reality, no more than those launched at Negro and Chinese immigrants during the same period. Equally, it was believed that the alien Jew was involved with crime. But in fact alien criminality was mostly to do with illicit financial

New Pavilion Theatre *c.*1910

Whitechapel was known for its Yiddish theatre. An article in the Graphic *in November 1889
explained that the Jews were 'very fond of the theatre'. Productions were of a biblical
or historical character such as* Joseph and His Brethren, Queen Esther and Haman
and Bar Cochba.

dealings, or the opening of workshops beyond the permitted hours. The alien Jew, in common with his British-born counterpart, was rarely found guilty of crimes of violence: a fact ignored by those who wished to identify the Ripper as of alien blood.

93

CONCLUSION

Although the Spitalfields Eastern European Jewish landscape of the 1880s did not specifically facilitate the Ripper, it did provide grounds for those who were convinced that, in the words of the *East London Observer*, 'it must have been done by a JEW'. Their visible otherness, the alien nature of their diet, their language and their religion, allied to the effects of their presence on the housing and job market, did much to harden the attitudes of those who, in the past, had been sympathetic to the newcomers. In addition there were those who maintained the tradition of religious anti-Jewishness and those, at a more intellectual level, who subscribed to theories of racial superiority and/or the rumours of Jewish plots to take over, if not the western world, then its economy. The vileness of the Ripper murders drove local residents and commentators to identify a culprit who was – indeed had to be – an outsider. Perhaps what is remarkable is not that a member of the immigrant Jewish community was suspected, but that the suspicions were not pursued for any length of time; they simply became part of the Jack the Ripper myth.

This is not to suggest that the Jewish East End was ephemeral. Its location on the landscape is embedded in more than just the local and transitory; it can be identified in the politics of the nation, in its economy, and in its cultural legacy. The mid-1880s concerns over the burgeoning number of sweatshops in the East End of London and their insanitary nature resulted in the House of Lords setting up a Sweating

☞ Petticoat Lane, c.1900

Londoners were drawn to Petticoat Lane on a Sunday morning especially for the clothes market. Here new and old garments were sold at very competitive prices. One reporter described the age of some of the clothes 'as indefinable as your favourite actress'. The market was dominated by Jewish stall holders and shopowners.

94

Commission in 1888, the year of the murders. Though initially the Commission's recommendations did little to ameliorate conditions and wages, the problem was recognised and pursued by further agitation and responding commissions in the twenty years that followed.[12] The outcome was the Trade Board Act of 1909 which set up a tripartite committee of employers, workers and trade unionists to determine minimum rates of pay in the four trades in which the worst examples of low wages – and thus sweating – prevailed. These were chain-making, lace-making, box-making and the ready-to-wear men's tailoring trade.

On the housing front, we have seen the way in which the Anglo-Jewish community and, some years later, the London County Council reacted to the severe conditions of overcrowding in the East End. However, the most significant piece of legislation to result from the Eastern European presence in the East End was the passage of the Aliens Act in 1905. The Act, which laid down the terms on which immigrants could enter the United Kingdom, was the first to come into operation in peacetime. It was a legislative response to the anti-alienist politicians, trade unionists, local residents of the East End and minority of overt anti-Semites[13] who wanted to see an end to pauper alien immigration and its deleterious effect on the economy and society. The Act was the forerunner of over a century of British immigration legislation.

The foregoing has dwelt on the negative but, as we have seen, there were success stories too. The Jewish East End provided London and the nation with writers and poets, among them Blumenfeld, Pinter, Rosenberg, Wesker and Zangwill; artists including Mark Gertler, and businessmen among whom can be counted Bernard Delfont and Lew Grade (brothers who grew up on the Boundary estate). Not all were born in the era of Jack the Ripper but they, and their parents, shared a heritage which – though to many it seemed bleak and lacking in opportunity – imbued them with a sense of ambition and instilled the ability to succeed. While Anglo-Jewry set out to 'iron out the ghetto bends', the immigrant community itself sought to integrate – while retaining its religious and cultural identity. As one son of immigrants who grew up in the first decades of the twentieth century told me, 'I just wanted to be an Englishman.' It took Hitler's bombs and the slum demolitions of the 1950s to reduce the vibrant Jewish East End to a memory and a resident community that could be counted in a few thousand rather than the tens of thousands of the 1880s.

NOTE

The Jewish East End is now 'Banglatown'. The resident immigrant population is Muslim and many attend prayers in the Jamme Masjid mosque on the corner of Brick Lane and Fournier Street that once was the ultra-orthodox Mazhike Hadath Synagogue.[14] Where once stood kosher butchers and poulterers there are now halal purveyors cheek by jowl with shops selling saris and skullcaps, religious music and Bollywood films. The smell of fried fish has been replaced by that of curry, and leather garments are now produced in what were the tailoring workshops of Hanbury and Fashion Streets. The new community is less eager to integrate, has no long-established hierarchy intent on the erosion of ethnic identity and arguably has become more, rather than less, entrenched in the ways of the outsider – the alien. But whatever the nature of the immigrant presence – and the Bengalis are now jostling for position with the newly arrived Eastern Europeans – the ghost of the Ripper remains.

CHAPTER THREE

LAW, ORDER AND VIOLENCE

Louise A. Jackson

Looking back on his early service in the Metropolitan Police, Frederick Porter Wensley characterised the late nineteenth century as 'a rougher and sterner age' and Whitechapel, where he had worked for 25 years, as one of the most brutal and violent districts. Its 'maze of ill-lighted alleys' was populated by 'the criminal classes' and 'infested by infamous women'. Drafted to Whitechapel in 1888 to patrol the streets with other reinforcements, Wensley rose through the ranks of the Criminal Investigations Department (CID) to act as its head before retiring in 1929. As he prepared his memoirs for publication he reinforced popular stereotypes of London's East End and its inhabitants as vicious and criminal. These stereotypes, developed by journalists and social investigators during the course of the nineteenth century, had been spectacularly paraded in the pages of Fleet Street newspapers as the events surrounding the Whitechapel murders were narrated to a rapt audience.

Petticoat Lane, c.1900

The vast crowds that gathered every Sunday morning in Middlesex Street also attracted pickpockets. Space was very confined on the pavements and in the roadway between the stalls. Here, two policemen patrol the market.

Wesley's own first impressions of the East End were inevitably shaped alongside this sensationalism. His later writings emphasise his role as 'hero' engaged in a quest against 'our native criminals and desperadoes', telling a story in which Whitechapel had been civilised to become a 'quiet and harmless district' by the late 1920s. Of course the stereotypes that linked the East End with a violent and criminal underworld lingered, requisitioned once again in press coverage and popular literature relating to the Kray twins and London's gangland of the 1960s. If we look beneath the sensationalism, however, we find that everyday experiences of violence and disorder were more mundane, although no less poignant.

THE WHEELS OF JUSTICE

The Metropolitan Police had been established by Sir Robert Peel in 1829, its principal object the systematic prevention of crime across the city. The new police were full-time and paid exclusively from the public purse in contrast to the previous combination of voluntary, private and parish-funded posts that had involved a range of constables, night watchmen and thief-takers. They were almost exclusively uniformed, with the original top hat and blue swallow-tailed coat replaced after 1863 with the well-known helmet and tunic of the 'bobby on the beat'. Undercover and detective policing developed from 1878 with the creation of the CID, the Whitechapel murders acting as an early test. The structure of the force was bureaucratic and hierarchical: it was headed by a Commissioner, who was answerable directly to the Home Secretary.

☞ Whitechapel, 1888
The implication of this Punch *cartoon is that all the police have been diverted to the streets of Whitechapel leaving the rest of the metropolis unpatrolled and easy picking for criminals.*

WHITECHAPEL, 1888.

FIRST MEMBER OF "CRIMINAL CLASS." "FINE BODY O' MEN, THE PER-LEECE!"
SECOND DITTO. "UNCOMMON FINE!—IT'S LUCKY FOR HUS AS THERE'S SECH A BLOOMIN' FEW ON 'EM!!!"

"I have to observe that the Metropolitan Police have not large reserves doing nothing and ready to meet emergencies; but every man has his duty assigned to him, and I can only strengthen the Whitechapel district by drawing men from duty in other parts of the Metropolis."—*Sir Charles Warren's Statement.* "There is one Policeman to every seven hundred persons."—*Vide Recent Statistics.*

By the late nineteenth century the Metropolitan Police District covered a radius of 15 miles centring on Charing Cross (only the square mile of the City of London lay outside its jurisdiction, with its own separate police force). It was divided into 21 land-based divisions, each identified by a letter of the alphabet, in addition to Thames Division, which covered the river itself. The notorious H Division of Whitechapel encompassed a discrete area of just 2 square miles, with police stations at Leman Street, Commercial Street, Stepney and Shadwell. To the north of this, Bethnal Green fell into the sprawling J Division of Hackney, which covered 40 square miles extending to Loughton in Essex. To the east, K Division of Bow (37 square miles) stretched along the northern banks of the Thames through Poplar and Dagenham, to Chadwell Heath and Purfleet. Whitechapel police division was bounded to the south by the river and to the west by the City. The period surrounding the Whitechapel murders saw a significant increase in manpower as the Metropolitan Police grew from an establishment of just under 7,000 officers in 1870 to nearly 16,000 in 1900.

Uniformed beat patrol was the central plank of preventative policing, designed to effect total surveillance of city space. Divisions were broken down into smaller and smaller units: stations, sections (of eight constables and a sergeant), and beats (patrol routes of no more than 1½ miles) to be covered day and night by a solitary police-man. The presence of uniformed officers acted as a deterrent to criminal activity. It also had a 'social cleansing' function. Public thoroughfares were to be cleared of obstructions that included drunks, vagrants, mischievous children, unlawful street traders and bookmakers. In their attempt to impose middle-class standards of

There was renewed public interest in the work of the police as the Whitechapel murders investigation unfolded. Here the Illustrated London News' *artist H.C. Seppings Wright depicted an identity parade and an arrest. The magazine recommended a small independent detective section in each police station in London.*

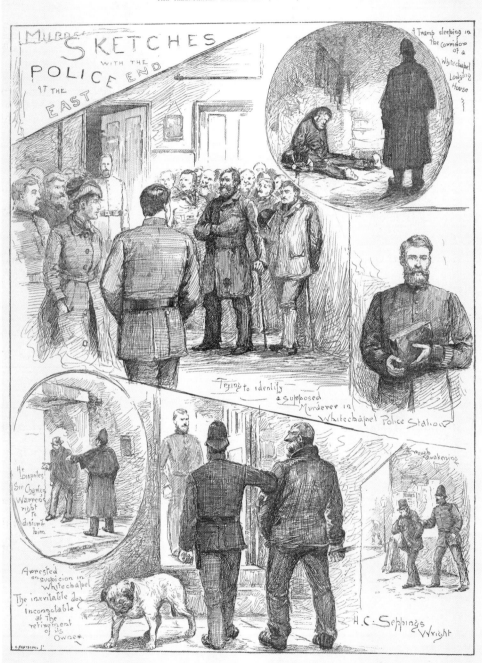

SKETCHES WITH THE POLICE AT THE EAST END

† Tramp sleeping in the corridor of a Whitechapel Lodging House

Trying to identify a supposed Murderer in Whitechapel Police Station

He Disputes Sir Charles Warren's right to disturb him

A rough awakening

Arrested on suspicion in Whitechapel

The inevitable dog Inconsolable at the retirement of its Owner.

H.C. Seppings Wright

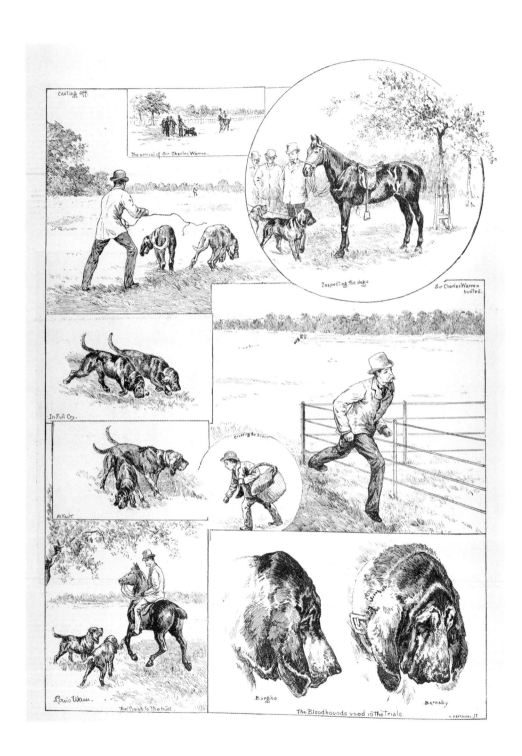

Casting off.

The arrival of Sir Charles Warren.

Inspecting the dogs

Sir Charles Warren hunted.

In Full Cry.

At Fault.

Crossing the scent

Louis Wain.

The Finish to the Duet.

Bungho

Barnaby

The Bloodhounds used in the Trials.

propriety, respectability and order upon public life, the new police have been described by R. D. Storch as 'a plague of blue locusts' waging war on traditional street culture by the mid-nineteenth century. Their allegiance with the ruling class was even more apparent at moments of crisis. Mounted police and life-guards brutally lashed into a crowd of unemployed labourers demonstrating in Trafalgar Square on 'Bloody Sunday', 13 November 1887, an incident still fresh in the minds of the London poor as the events of 1888 unfolded.

Yet the class position of the London 'bobby' was contradictory, the power dynamics by no means one-sided. To avoid conflicts of loyalty, officers were recruited, where possible, as 'outsiders'. Research by H. Shpayer-Makov has shown that between 1889 and 1909 only 28 per cent of recruits were Londoners. Frederick Wensley had grown up in Taunton, Somerset, before joining the Metropolitan Police in 1887 at the age of 22. Disciplinary mechanisms aimed to establish a standard of civility and sobriety (officers were sacked for drunkenness). Yet wages were low. By 1890 constables received a similar wage to unskilled labourers while sergeants' pay was comparable to that of skilled artisans. Most policemen were drawn from ordinary working-class backgrounds. They had considerable sympathy for popular pastimes such as street gambling, which they believed to be harmless (some may have warned bookmakers of raids in advance). According to Shpayer-Makov, by the late nineteenth century 'a form of "truce" had developed between the respectable working class and the police'. However, a heavy-handed approach was still taken towards the city's lumpenproletariat: 'the poor, casual labourers, vagrants, prostitutes and drunks'.

Louis Wain's drawings capture Sir Charles Warren being tracked by Barnaby and Burgho, two bloodhounds, across Hyde Park. Some experts felt that dogs could be used to track the killer if properly trained but others mocked the Commissioner of the Metropolitan Police for even considering their use.

Given the extent of poverty in its midst, Whitechapel could be viewed as something of a front line. Wensley stated that its inhabitants 'considered they had a natural right to get fighting and knock a policeman about whenever the spirit moved him'. Police surveillance was frustrated by the layout of alleys and courts. While the wide thoroughfares of Commercial Road and Whitechapel High Street were lined with shops and offices run by an affluent middle class, pockets of back-street housing took on the nature of ghettos, which the police entered with trepidation. The Flower and Dean Street rookery, infamous for its cheap lodging-houses (and associated with all of the women assumed to be Ripper victims), was viewed as unsafe for police officers to enter alone due to high levels of assault. A local newspaper, the *Tower Hamlets Independent*, reported in 1882 that it was 'useless for the police to follow beyond a certain point, even when they happen to appear on the scene, as the houses communicate with one another and a man pursued can run in and out, like a rabbit in a warren'. Just north of this, the area of the Nichol, bounded by High Street, Shoreditch, and Spitalfields, was described by former resident Arthur Harding as bearing an 'evil reputation'. The inability of the police to catch the Whitechapel assassin exposed the limitations of the uniform beat system, leading to the resignation of Commissioner Warren, head of the Metropolitan Police in November 1888.

Yet the characterisation of Whitechapel and surrounding areas as a lawless terrain in which the mechanisms of criminal justice struggled to exert control requires further scrutiny. As well as enforcing law and order, policemen also performed a social role; Harding explains that, as a 'missing child', he had been made a 'fuss of' at the police station: 'they'd give you a slice of bread and jam . . . they usually had a

Policeman with lost child, c.1905

Police constables on their patrols through the streets of London performed social duties by helping children who had lost their way or had been separated from their parents.

BLIND-MAN'S BUFF.

(As played by the Police.)

"TURN ROUND THREE TIMES,
AND CATCH WHOM YOU MAY!"

IS DETECTION A FAILURE?

In the interests of the Gutter Gazette and of the Criminal Classes, the Sensational Interviewer dogs the Detective's footsteps, and throws the strong light of publicity on his work. Under these circumstances, it is not surprising that Detection should prove a failure.

'Is detection a failure?' *Punch*, 20 October 1888

Before the days of press conferences, the police revealed very little about their investigation into catching the Whitechapel murderer. It was left to eager reporters to unearth new information. They interviewed witnesses and published a range of theories about the identity of the killer. Harry Furniss' cartoon implied that they also hindered the investigation and helped the murderer by tracking the work of the detectives.

Blind-man's buff. *Punch*, 22 September 1888

The poem accompanying this illustration explained that the police ('sleuthhounds') were 'at fault . . . Blundering around without a settled aim/ Like boys at Blind-Man's Buff.'

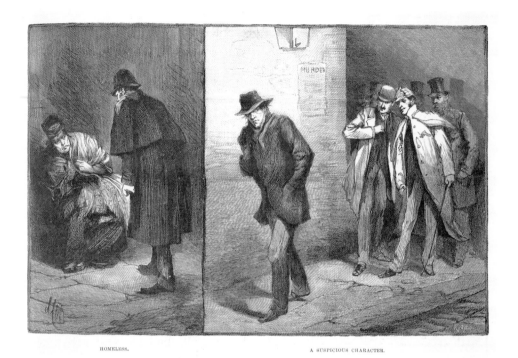

HOMELESS.   A SUSPICIOUS CHARACTER.

A local 'vigilance committee' was formed to work with the police in patrolling the streets at night.
Sometimes confusion occurred when plain clothes officers drafted in from other parts of London
were followed and stopped by locals. Another fear for the police and 'vigilance committee' was the
murderer might be carrying a revolver and would defend himself if approached.

couple of toys.' Over time, police officers patrolling the beat built up relationships
with the 'regulars'. Moreover, the police did not operate in isolation. They worked
very closely with another institution of law enforcement, the magistracy, who sat
in London's police courts. Set up in 1792, police court jurisdictions covered slightly
different areas to those of the newer police divisions. By the 1880s Whitechapel and
the wider East End were covered by two courts. Worship Street police court took

Thames police court, *c.*1902

Jack London when he visited the courtroom was astonished by the speed in which cases were heard and sentences passed. He witnessed 'drunks, disorderlies, vagrants, brawlers, wife-beaters, thieves, fences, gamblers, and women of the street' stepping in and out of the dock 'in a stream as steady as the stream of sentences which fell from the magistrate's lips'.

business relating to the northern part of Whitechapel, Spitalfields, Shoreditch and Bethnal Green; it included the rookeries of both Flower and Dean Street and the Nichol. The district to the south of Aldgate and the Commercial Road, including the southern limits of Whitechapel as well as Limehouse, came under the jurisdiction of Thames police court, situated in East Arbour Street, Stepney. Magistrates were the gatekeepers of the wider criminal justice system. All of those charged with offences, no matter how minor, were brought before a magistrate for an initial hearing. A case might be dismissed, dealt with by means of a fine or short prison sentence, or referred to the Quarter Sessions or Central Criminal Court at the Old Bailey if the matter was so serious that it could only be tried by jury.

Unlike other areas of the country where summary justice was dispensed by amateur and unpaid Justices of the Peace, the stipendiary magistrates who were paid to oversee London's police courts were professional barristers of extensive experience. Like judges, however, they gained a personal reputation for being 'lenient' or 'strict'. Montagu Williams QC (1835–92) had undertaken a highly successful 25-year career as defence counsel at the Old Bailey before his appointment as a Metropolitan magistrate by the Home Secretary in 1886. Working initially in Greenwich and Woolwich, he arrived at Worship Street in the summer of 1888. In the midst of the Whitechapel murders he was deeply aware of 'the possibility of the assassin, if arrested, being brought before me' and he took care 'to personally visit all the scenes of the crimes, and to make what medical and other inquiries' he thought necessary. He hinted that he knew who the murderer was, but drew short of outlining his theories in his published memoirs.

Closely involved with the daily life of the urban poor, Williams gained a reputation for paternalism and was described as 'the poor man's magistrate' in his *Times* obituary of 24 December 1892. While complaining of the immorality of the East End poor, Williams blamed it on poverty and degradation rather than hereditary disposition; during the severe winter of 1891 he set up a depot for the relief of distress in the Thames and Worship Street police court districts, asking for donations of blankets and clothing from wealthier residents. He made use of the police in his quest to civilise the East End. Disturbed by the grotesque waxworks exhibitions and peep-shows depicting the Whitechapel murders that had sprung up as huge crowd-pullers, he encouraged the police to prosecute showmen for causing a public

THE UNEMPLOYED AT THE EAST-END OF LONDON: APPLICANTS FOR THE RELIEF FUND.

The unemployed at the East-End of London, *Illustrated London News*, 27 March 1886
This wood engraving by Mathew Morgan shows poor people queuing up to receive relief from the
Mansion House Fund. Applicants had to be assessed before money was given out.

obstruction. Yet he also saw himself as maintaining a position of detached objectivity
with regard to police evidence. This was characterised by his detractors, such as
Chartres Biron, as over-critical: 'he had developed a suspicion of police evidence
which had, at times, an unfortunate effect. A good many ruffians got off whom the
police thought should have been convicted.' Williams was not alone in this. The
elderly and far less popular Thames magistrate Thomas William Saunders, described
as 'formidable' and as 'the hammer of vagrants and foreigners' by Fishman, viewed

police evidence with equal caution. A memoir attributed to him comments that the police had a tendency of 'supplementing their evidence when the charge is inherently weak, by the allegation that the defendant is a well-known bad character, or is the terror of the neighbourhood, or associate of roughs'. Magistrates were warned to exercise 'only the most watchful and scrutinizing care'. The police and magistracy presented by no means a united front, and 'justice' involved considerable discretion.

The London police courts, including Thames and Worship Street, played an important role in the lives of the urban poor, offering charity, advice, support, and a means to solve interpersonal disputes. They could be used by ordinary people to enforce the moral codes of their own communities. Ultimately, however, they were acting in judgement on the London poor, who were far more likely than the rich to become the objects of prosecution.

ORDER AND MORALITY

A survey of the cases recorded in the Thames police court registers in the late summer of 1888 sheds light on the relationship between police, magistracy and local community.[1] The business of the courts was extensive. Two magistrates were assigned to each court and the court met six days a week, dealing with anything between 20 and 60 defendants each day, commencing with the 'night charges' involving those whom the police had taken into custody overnight. In the months of July, August and September 1888 a total of 2,174 defendants appeared before Thames police court magistrates Thomas Saunders and Frederick Lushington (with Montagu Williams covering for Lushington in the last week of July). Around 30 per cent of cases involved public order offences, 27 per cent involved interpersonal violence (including assault of various forms), 23 per cent concerned property (including theft, receiving stolen property, and fraud), while a further 20 per cent of the cases involved miscellaneous offences such as

Outside an East End music hall, *c.*1890

*Music halls were a very popular form of entertainment in the East End. Many social
and religious reformers saw them as centres of vice and immorality. Drunkenness and brawling
was a common sight on the streets outside the music halls and public houses.*

street gambling, begging, bigamy, cruelty to animals or deserting the army. This should
not be viewed as a simple indication of 'criminal' behaviour. Patterns of prosecution
reflect policing priorities and the enthusiasm of local residents to use the law to resolve
disputes, although these responses may be shaped by actual offending.

The largest category of cases (around 30 per cent) involved minor public order
offences, mostly related to drunkenness; these included charges of 'drunk and
incapable', 'drunk and disorderly' and 'drunk, disorderly and using bad language'.[2]

The White Hart public house, Bethnal Green Road, *c*.1900
Groups of women were often to be seen standing on the pavement outside pubs in the East End.
It was more respectable for women to drink outside. Here, four women, with elaborate hats,
chat to each other, one with a baby in her arms and another looking after two children.
They have placed their beer glasses on the ledge of the pub's window.

☞   Brewery Tap, Whitechapel Road, *c*.1900
For the temperance movement drink was an evil. The poor squandered their meagre wages
on beer and gin. As a consequence, they failed to feed or clothe their children adequately.
Domestic violence was another disturbing feature of alcoholism.

Concerns about the drink problem in the East End and its relationship to other forms of offending behaviour were regularly voiced by social commentators. It was a social problem that was identified as widespread among women as well as men. Criminality was associated with masculinity in Victorian minds, since women tended to appear before the courts in far fewer numbers, constituting around a fifth of those charged with both indictable and petty offences between 1850 and 1900. At Thames police court, however, women formed over a quarter of all defendants in the late summer of 1888 (27 per cent). This figure was spectacularly enhanced by their prosecution for drink-related public order offences: women formed nearly half (46 per cent) of all those charged with this type of offence at East Arbour Street, compared to a presence of just over a third in national profiles of summary offences.

All of the women identified as victims of the Whitechapel murderer were heavy drinkers and involved in prostitution; alcohol was a coping mechanism as well as an exacerbating factor in lives structured by real poverty and insecurity. The killer's third victim, Elizabeth Stride, aged around 45, was well known to East Arbour Street magistrates. Court registers suggest she was discharged by Mr Lushington for being drunk, disorderly and using obscene language on 16 July 1888; she was named as being fined 5 shillings for a similar offence by Mr Saunders on 8 August. On 3 August she appears to have failed to answer a summons for being drunk and incapable. Similarly, a 22-year-old woman named Mary Jane Kelley (*sic*), who was fined 2s. 6d. for drunk and disorderly behaviour on 19 September, may be the same Mary Jane (or Mary Ann) Kelly who died in Miller's Court on 9 November. Catherine Eddowes, who was murdered in Mitre Square, Aldgate, was reputedly making her way back to her lodging-house in Flower and Dean Street after being discharged from Bishopsgate police station where she had been detained for drunkenness by the City of London Police.[3] It is often argued that women's association with domesticity and the private space of the home meant that they were less likely to become visibly

Itchy Park, *c.*1900

Just to the south of Christ Church, Spitalfields, was a small park that once had been a
graveyard. Locked and empty at night, by day it was full of homeless men and women who were
slumped on the hard benches. Jack London was horrified by what he saw:
'On the benches on either side was arrayed a mass of miserable and distorted humanity
... a welter of rags and filth, of all manner of loathsome skin diseases, open sores, bruises,
grossness, indecency, leering monstrosities, and bestial faces. A chill, raw wind was blowing, and
these creatures huddled there in their rags, sleeping for the most part, or trying to sleep.'

119

involved in criminality. The overtly 'public' worlds of Whitechapel's destitute women, who inhabited the streets, sleeping rough or making use of lodging-houses, brought them under close scrutiny and into frequent contact with the police.

The East End was widely associated with prostitution, Whitechapel Road being likened by W. Goldman to an 'open-air brothel'. Yet prosecutions of individual women for prostitution-related offences were surprisingly low. Under Victorian legislation, soliciting was not itself illegal. The 1824 Vagrancy Act punished any 'common prostitute' who behaved 'in a riotous or indecent manner' in a public place with one month's imprisonment for a first offence. The 1839 Metropolitan Police Act stipulated that a 'common prostitute or night-walker' loitering or soliciting in a public place 'to the annoyance of the inhabitants or passers-by' could be fined 40 shillings.

The term 'common prostitute' was open to interpretation, although it was some-times linked to previous police cautions. Magistrates were reluctant to convict on police evidence alone and 'inhabitants or passers-by' were rarely willing to appear as court witnesses. A high-profile case of 1887, in which a Miss Elizabeth Cass had been incorrectly arrested in Regent Street by Constable Endacott, led to public outcry and criticism of police methods. It was felt that the police should not act as moral censors; rather, as the 1824 and 1839 legislation suggested, their concern was public nuisance. Subsequently the police adopted a more laissez-faire approach. A total of 2,797 women were arrested for prostitution-related offences across the metropolis in 1888, less than half the annual figure before the Cass case. Only two women were charged at Thames police court between July and September. Both appeared before Mr Lushington together on 9 August: Julia Lefair, aged 29, was discharged while Ellen Mansfield, aged 27, was sentenced to 14 days' hard labour. It is likely that police arrests tended to centre on the main thoroughfares of the West End, where street-walkers shared the pavements with 'respectable' shoppers and theatre-goers, rather than the more proletarian environment of east London. Given widespread poverty in Whitechapel, women's resort to prostitution in times of hardship, as part of an 'economy of make-shifts', may have been viewed with some acceptance and sympathy by neighbours, as well as by police and magistrates.[4] Indeed, there was a barely discernible line between the financial trans-action associated with prostitution and other forms of sexual barter in which women exchanged sex for food or gifts with men they knew.

A lodging-house keeper,
Flower and Dean Street,
Spitalfields, *c.*1900

The Criminal Law Amendment Act of 1885 gave parish vestries the authority to prosecute brothel keepers and to approach the police for assistance in securing evidence. Yet, despite knowledge that the common lodging-houses in Flower and Dean Street were used for the purposes of prostitution, little concerted action appears to have been taken against them. Lodging-house keepers made an income from renting beds or rooms and from providing food and drink for customers. The two prosecutions for brothel-keeping that took place at Thames police court in September 1888 appear to have involved households based around husband and wife teams. Brothels on the Continent appear to have been regulated, but those in the East End seem to have lacked any overall organisation.

Police and magistrates were aware of 'bullies' and 'roughs' who attempted to extort money from women engaged in prostitution. As a young lawyer, Montagu Williams had successfully prosecuted Francis Jones for brutally assaulting Georgina Evans. Jones had been described as the 'Terror of the Haymarket' for threatening 'the poor creatures' who solicited around the West End theatres. An early police theory, subsequently abandoned, suggested the Whitechapel murders were the work of a gang of blackmailing ruffians. The brutal treatment of women involved in prostitution was evidenced in the police courts on a daily basis. In July 1888 Edith Brockwell, who described herself as 'an unfortunate', accused Philip Leman, 'a brothel-keeper' with whom she lodged near East India Dock, of assault. Her injuries had been treated at the London Hospital and she attended court with her nose in plaster, stating that 'he punched her about the face, knocked her down, kicked her and afterwards held her by the throat until she was exhausted'. In mid-September 1888 a Limehouse woman was stabbed in the head outside the Coach and Horses beershop by a Japanese man who told her 'if you run away from me tonight I will rip you up the same way as the woman was served in the Whitechapel Road'.[5] The Whitechapel murders can be seen as part of a continuum of violent assaults on women engaged in prostitution. While there is considerable evidence of female support networks, male bullies and pimps were clearly operating in the East End, particularly around the docks. It was the replacement of lodging-houses with model dwellings (such as Rothschild Buildings in Flower and Dean Street) that led to a reduction in prostitution in Whitechapel, rather than any intensification of the law or policing. Yet the Dorset Street area continued to be associated with prostitution well into the twentieth century.

ASSAULT AND DOMESTIC VIOLENCE

After public order offences related to drunkenness, cases of interpersonal violence formed the next-largest category – involving 27 per cent of defendants – at Thames police court between July and September 1888. Nearly a quarter of these were charges of assaulting a police officer; most appear to have arisen from attempts to resist arrest for other offences, or by onlookers assisting these attempts. Most accounts suggest that the inhabitants of the East End were quick to resort to violence to protect themselves and others. Policemen needed to be tough to command authority; the rough and tumble of street life created a more robust style of policing than was later to be considered acceptable. It is possible that the concept of a 'fair fight' was viewed by both parties as part of the process of securing an arrest. The *Metropolitan Police Instruction Book* advocated 'no more violence . . . than is absolutely necessary'. If arrest was resisted, officers should arm-lock the prisoner; as a last resort, a truncheon could be aimed at the arms and legs. The physicality of policing is emphasised in police memoirs. Ben Leeson, who served in Whitechapel in the 1890s, was called to a public house to arrest a sailor:

> I was lifted up bodily and thrown over the counter . . . we indulged in a 'slow motion' wrestling match . . . 'Why don't you use your stick?' said the [section] sergeant. 'What d'yer think it's for?' With that he drew his truncheon and tapped the sailor on the head. In a moment the whole lot set on us, and it was then that I used my truncheon for the first time, and effectively too.

On rare occasions police brutality resulted in formal complaint; in 1908 PC Edwin Ashworth was found guilty of an assault on George Gamble in Whitechapel. Arthur Harding, who was involved in a range of offences from pickpocketing to racketeering and gun crime in the early part of the twentieth century, described the police as a combination of 'proper policemen' and 'bullying types' or 'villains': 'they put me away for things I didn't do as well as for what I did.' Yet the 'proper police-men' of his narratives come across as generous, humane, and friendly towards those on their local patch. Policing styles varied enormously, but physical toughness was necessary for survival in the job. Magistrates made it clear that assaults on police officers would be dealt with seriously, Montagu Williams insisting on a prison sentence of eight days for each offence.

Although Victorian criminal justice has been viewed by M. Wiener as a 'civilising mission' to tame the rough and pugilistic masculinity associated with the 'lower orders', its successes were distinctly limited in Whitechapel. Domestic violence, particularly assaults by men on wives and girlfriends, were extremely common according to contemporary commentators such as Harding: 'Husbands of the working class were very ignorant and brutal in their treatment of their women, and . . . I often saw the results of a row upon my mother's face.' Court registers indicate that at least 6 per cent of the assault cases heard by Thames magistrates between July and September 1888 involved family violence, given that complainants and defendants shared surnames. Three cases were of husbands alleging violence by their wives; two custodial sentences were given, while one case was discharged after the complainant failed to appear. The majority of cases (26) involved complaints of brutal treatment made by wives against husbands.[6] In half of these cases the defendant was discharged; custodial sentences were passed in six cases. It is likely that domestic violence was one of the most under-reported of offences, in large part because the mechanisms of criminal justice offered few practical solutions for the marital difficulties of the urban poor.

In addition to hearing criminal charges, magistrates heard a range of requests for advice from East End residents and applications for summonses against third parties.

124

The seamy side of life: behind a pawnbroker's counter, *c.*1890

The counter area of a pawnbroker was often divided into compartments or 'boxes' offering some privacy to customers. Pledged items were packaged in bundles identifiable by a ticket and stored above or behind the shop counter. Items not redeemed within twelve months became the property of the pawnbroker and could be sold.

These included complaints against pawnbrokers and employers for withholding goods or wages, but also requests from married women for 'protection orders' against violent husbands. As Williams frequently pointed out, no such order existed. Reporting domestic violence could create further problems. If wives chose to take out a summons against a husband for violent assault they faced the possibility of losing a

male breadwinner if he was sent to prison, as well as recriminations and further marital breakdown when he returned home. These difficulties may explain the high number of discharges, as magistrates felt it was not in the woman's best interests to punish a defendant. Wives often took out summonses against husbands but failed to appear to support their charges when they realised the possible implications. The Matrimonial Causes Act of 1878 offered a further solution, giving magistrates powers to grant separation orders in cases of cruelty. In order to invoke the cruelty clause a magistrate not only had to convict the defendant but to be satisfied 'that the future safety of the wife is in peril', according to the author of *Metropolitan Police Court Jottings*. Three separation orders were granted in this way at Thames police court in a three-month period; in a further three cases husbands were bound over to be of good behaviour. Women's acute experiences of brutality and poverty may also explain their dominant presence in figures for attempted suicide (15 of 18 cases coming before magistrates between July and September 1888). Cycles of violence, self-harm and alcohol abuse were interlinked.

High levels of violence between men and women were not unique to the East End of London. Assumptions that violence was not part and parcel of the middle-class family were rarely questioned. It was the home life of the poor, rather than the rich, which was subject to investigation, surveillance and censure as a result of the activities of new bodies of police officers, voluntary social workers, School Board officials and child welfare inspectors. Living in close proximity to one another, East End neighbours were conscious of the ways in which family relationships were

Women wait at 7.30 a.m. for the pawnbrokers Phillips and Scoones (263 Cambridge Road, Bethnal Green) to open at 8 a.m. on a Monday morning. The three golden balls sign was familiar throughout the East End. Many poor people pawned their belongings to tide them over during the week until they had earned some money.

conducted; any notion of privacy was severely curtailed as relationships were played out on the street or in front of lodgers, friends and kin. The challenges presented by poverty, overcrowding and resort to alcohol exacerbated tensions within family life, although domestic violence was by no means exclusive to the poor. Rows between husbands and wives often escalated as both parties were fuelled by drink. It is striking, however, that, by the late nineteenth century, poor women in London believed they had a right to seek protection and made use of the courts to complain about domestic violence even though the law did not always provide the solution they wanted. In July 1888 Montagu Williams told 19-year-old William Donovan: 'you have committed a brutal assault on your sister and given her a frightful black eye. She asks me simply to bind you over to keep the peace, but I shall not listen to that. You will go to prison for six weeks with hard labour.' In another case during the same month, Rebecca Janowski appeared in court to give evidence against her husband, Jacob, despite needing a translator and despite being in 'a very weak condition'.[7] The poor used the courts with knowledge and confidence to seek redress for wrongs.

SEXUAL VIOLENCE

The Whitechapel murders were widely discussed by early criminologists and sexologists as examples of extreme sexual 'perversion' as well as physical brutality. Again, the East End was presented as their inevitable home because of its association with vice, degradation and immorality. As has already been shown, low-level violence between men and women was an everyday occurrence, although not specific to Whitechapel or to the poor. Cases of sexual assault figured in the courts with far less frequency. In order to examine the way in which it was dealt with by the courts as well as the perceptions and responses of the wider community, a broader sample has been constructed of all sexual assault cases referred to Thames police court for the years

The Whitechapel Monster seen by two men, *Illustrated Police News*, 20 October 1888
Although the engraving is directed to the identity of Jack the Ripper, the image also shows East
End prostitution. Men met prostitutes on the streets. Sex was a commodity that could be bought.
For women prostitution was a way of earning a living.

1885, 1890, 1895 and 1900 (66 cases in total); a broad range of newspaper reports has
also been consulted.[8] A number of trends are striking, including the significance of
London's police courts in the decision-making process. The majority (60 per cent)
were dealt with purely by magistrates, who either discharged the defendants or
convicted them of the lesser charge of common assault (sexual assault cases could

only be tried by judge and jury). Also apparent is the high proportion of victims who were minors: female children under the age of consent (fixed at 16 in 1885) constituted at least two-thirds of all victims, while only 5 per cent of cases are known to have involved adult women.[9] A third striking trend is that a minority of cases (42 per cent) resulted in a conviction of any sort. How should we make sense of these findings?

We should not assume that sexual violence against women was uncommon, despite its low presence here. Nor should we assume that the sexual abuse of children was widespread and condoned in the East End, given its high representation. Instead, mothers were much more likely to approach magistrates and police about abuse of their daughters than about assaults on themselves. Child abuse was condemned even among the very poor, and East End communities subscribed to their own ethical and moral frameworks. The courts considered sexual violence one of the most serious of all offences; yet they were extremely reluctant to convict because the inevitable secrecy, surrounding child abuse in particular, meant that the testimony of victims was rarely corroborated.

In *The Bitter Cry of Outcast London* of 1883 the Reverend Andrew Mearns had stated that 'incest' was 'common' among the urban poor because of overcrowded sleeping arrangements when whole families shared one room. These comments were echoed by Lord Shaftesbury. Those who disagreed received less publicity. The Reverend Alfred Fryer, a Clerkenwell vicar, told the 1884 Royal Commission on the Housing of the Working Classes that although London children were knowledgeable about the realities of sexuality and pregnancy, this did not mean they were abused, corrupted or immoral. Rooms were often partitioned with curtains to preserve a sense of personal modesty. Arthur Harding argued that 'children were well respected in the East End'. Girls in their early teens 'had an upbringing that prevented them from being ever interfered with', warned by their mothers to stick together and to avoid contact with strangers when out on errands in the evening.

Even among the residents of the common lodging-houses of Flower and Dean Street, a shared moral code condemned the abuse of children, as is demonstrated by a striking case in which a nine-year-old girl, daughter of a city grocer, had gone missing in 1865.[10] There was no trace of her for a week, until she was found as a patient in the London Hospital, Whitechapel Road. She had been decoyed and abducted by a labourer, who had forced her to wander the streets. At night they slept in lodging-houses, the child sharing a bed with the landlady's little girl. One evening, the man had taken her to a house in Flower and Dean Street, where

The depictions of Jack the Ripper's murdered victims in popular illustrated newspapers, such as here in the Illustrated Police News *(6 October 1888), implied the prevalence of brutal behaviour towards women in the East End.*

he asked an Irishwoman in charge for a double bed. She refused, told him the child must sleep with one of the female servants, and asked 'him if he was not ashamed of himself'. Residents took the law into their own hands: 'some of the lodgers indignant at the prisoner bringing the child there, set upon him and struck him, upon which he ran out of the house leaving the child behind.' They took the child to hospital and summoned the police, who arrested the man in a crowd.

Cases such as this demonstrate the power of neighbourhood sanctions, including community violence or ostracisation, as well as a desire to use the law when

131

considered necessary. Overcrowded neighbourhoods had their own moral codes and sensibilities, and the poor refused to tolerate those who disregarded them. Pimping and other forms of exploitation were similarly looked upon with condemnation. In May 1880 a female mob had gathered outside Thames police court, threatening to lynch a German man alleged to have forced a young woman into prostitution (the case had been discharged by the magistrate).[11] Where the law failed to resolve the matter, 'rough justice' was invoked, requiring further police intervention.

Cases of the sexual abuse of girls often involved men they knew. In September 1870 a 22-year-old grocer's assistant was sent to prison for two years for indecently assaulting the seven-year-old daughter of his employers, who ran a shop in Cable Street: 'the parents of the girl are honest and industrious people and, believing the prisoner to be a respectable and moral man, allowed their daughter to be continually with him.'[12] Shared residential spaces such as yards and water closets brought neighbours and children into close proximity; for some this might create opportunities for abuse. Mothers and other female relatives often played a prominent role in tracking down an alleged assailant and giving him into custody. In April 1870 a mother went in pursuit of a neighbour after her eight-year-old daughter complained that he had assaulted her in a shared water closet in Spring Gardens. She told the magistrate at Worship Street: 'I went to the prisoner's house, saw him & asked how dare he take such a liberty with my child.'[13] Children from Whitechapel and Bethnal Green who walked up to Victoria Park, Hackney, to play were watched carefully by park keepers who referred miscreants to the police. Local residents who witnessed suspicious behaviour in the street might also intervene, necessitating one defendant to go into a fruiterer's shop and give 'the owner his watch and chain in order to protect himself and property from the crowd that had assembled'.[14] Londoners policed their own moral boundaries.

Public debate on sexual violence was largely framed in terms of a moral panic about the existence of a 'white slave trade'. Emotive and melodramatic, this drew on the language of race to suggest the internationally organised entrapment and rape of young white women by 'foreign' men who then forced them into prostitution. In the 1870s it had been claimed that English girls were being lured to Belgium. In the 1880s concerns were voiced about the fate that awaited English 'maidens' in the labyrinth of the London streets. The influx of Jewish refugees into the East End in this decade also raised anxieties about Eastern European men preying on Jewish girls. Officers employed by the Jewish Association for the Protection of Women and Children met boats as they arrived at the docks and escorted single women and girls to safe accommodation. Thus 'white slavery' was recast as a Jewish problem. By the early years of the twentieth century, Whitechapel was still viewed as the 'lair of these traffickers', who now had links to South America. In his *Memoirs of an East-End Detective*, Ben Leeson explained how he had taken a statement from a 16-year-old Jewish schoolgirl who said she had become 'a white slave victim, falling into the hands of a man who took her to Buenos Ayres, where she was sold for £250'. She was spotted in South America by the British Consul, who arranged for her return home. Within a few weeks she had disappeared to set up home with her alleged abductor, against whom she refused to give evidence; the couple later married. To what extent she was the victim of organised trafficking is difficult to discern.

Single immigrant women, unable to speak English, were undoubtedly in a position of vulnerability if they did not have a close network of family and friends to fall back on. In August 1888 a tailor's machinist, Nathan Reuben, had been charged with 'detaining a Polish woman, named Anne Goldstein, for immoral purposes'. Goldstein said she had been in London for four months, living first with relatives and then attempting to find a place in service. She seems to have turned to Reuben, who had been introduced to her by a third party, because he promised her food and a roof over her head. She alleged he had brought a man into her room one day and locked them in.[15] There was little substantive evidence to suggest the existence of professionalised criminal networks organising international trafficking. Ultimately, the concept of 'the white slave trade' must be viewed as another exotic myth associated with Whitechapel, grounded in reality but distorted for effect. Its 'truth' lay in its essence – exploitation – rather than in its detailed substance. As Anne Goldstein's plight suggests, the mistreatment of women – by men they knew rather than by 'foreigners' – was a mundane fact of everyday life for many.

THE VIOLENT EAST END: CONSTRUCTION OF A MYTH

If Whitechapel was stereotyped for good reason as 'violent', its inhabitants demonstrated their own shared sense of justice and fair play. There is also a sense in which they used black humour to parody its reputation. Arriving in Whitechapel in 1890 as a 'rookie' policeman, Ben Leeson found himself lost on his first trip out alone: 'I was compelled to ask my way, which brought down on my head a torrent of more or less good-natured abuse, such as "copper lost his way", "do him in", "we kill all coppers who come down this street" and so forth.' In encounters such as this, the disjuncture of myth and reality was exposed. Frederick Wensley claimed that dead bodies were regularly found in Whitechapel and that busy coroners rarely bothered to establish whether they were victims of murder unless there was 'obvious evidence of foul play'. Without detailed inquest reports it is difficult to establish whether this was yet another urban myth about the 'dangerous classes' of the East End, embellished by police culture and popular rumour. The persistent presence of the Metropolitan Police, as well as the rebuilding of whole sections of the district, mean that Whitechapel probably was 'less' violent in 1900 than in 1880.

Both the police and 'known criminals' like Arthur Harding represented criminality in the East End as an 'underworld' of activity, structured around clearly defined armed gangs involved in forms of racketeering. 'Outlaws' and detectives are presented as locked in a battle for control over the East End. Yet this model does not account for the vast majority of offences (mostly minor ones) tried in the police courts, nor for the majority of police time, which was taken up with preventative uniform beat patrol rather than the detective work of 'thief-taking'. While there was a respectable middle and working class in Whitechapel and the surrounding area, who could afford to maintain an image as law-abiding, the experience of poverty meant this was unattainable for many. The East End poor participated in a range of white, grey and black economies as part of a survival strategy. For women this might include soliciting, for children, the thieving of small items of food from stalls. The central role played by the pawnshop in most family budgets might encourage transactions that were on the edges of legality. Disputes were aired in the police court when lodgers 'borrowed' items from rented rooms or employers to pawn for cash.[16] Although Whitechapel had more than its fair share of burglaries, most criminal activity was less glamorous and less organised than the mythic term 'underworld' suggests. What is clear, however, is that the East End poor were enterprising in their use of networks of family and kin, and resourceful in their adoption of a broad range of strategies for getting by. They preserved their own moral guidelines of right and wrong, which did not always sit comfortably with the mechanisms of criminal justice. Violence and brutality were part and parcel of everyday slum living in the late nineteenth century but they were not confined to Whitechapel. The Whitechapel murders took place in a context in which male violence to women was still endemic although not necessarily accepted – either by those who viewed themselves as 'respectable' or by poor women, their female neighbours and relations.

Sclater Street bird market, *c.*1900

Mrs Robinson, stuffing mattresses at home in her back yard, *c.*1900

John Galt, a missionary, photographed both the back yards of people's houses as well as the streets of Whitechapel and Bethnal Green. He aimed to show the dignity and humanity of those living in the slums of the East End, revealing that they were worthy of salvation. Mrs Robinson received one shilling for each completed mattress. Thousands of caged birds were displayed for sale in Sclater Street, to the north of Brick Lane, each Sunday.

A market stall, *c.*1900

The East End was known for its vibrant street markets with hundreds of temporary stalls and barrows. Houndsditch Market was where the cheapest fresh fruit and nuts could be bought and Petticoat Lane the centre of the old clothes trade. Along Whitechapel High Street small traders sold all manner of cheap goods such as ribbons, hairpins, woollen and cotton garments, pipes, furs, pins, cigars, fresh fish and vegetables. The air was filled with the smells of the produce and the cries of the vendors.

Two blind street musicians performing in the East End, *c.*1900

London streets were busy, noisy places. The cries of street traders competed with the barrel organ and the busker. Popular tunes played by gifted blind street musicians were some of the more pleasant sounds that pedestrians heard as they went about their day-to-day business.

CHAPTER FOUR

COMMON LODGINGS AND 'FURNISHED ROOMS': HOUSING IN 1880s WHITECHAPEL

RICHARD DENNIS

Held Dante's Circles such a dwelling-place?
Did primal sludge e'er harbour such a race?

Slum-farming knaves suck shameful wealth from sin,
But a dread Nemesis abides therein.

(from *Punch, or the London Charivari*, 29 September 1888)

The moral panic associated with the Whitechapel murders needs to be set in the context of at least three other panics, each of which directs our attention to the nature of housing – its physical and social condition, its cost, its ownership and management.

In 1883 Andrew Mearns had produced his famous tract, *The Bitter Cry of Outcast London*, scandalising polite society with claims that incest was rife in one-room dwellings in the slums of south-east London. Meanwhile, a more sober debate about

Little Collingwood Street, Bethnal Green, *c*.1900

housing conditions and government policy, initiated by a review of the Torrens and Cross Acts, slum clearance legislation introduced in 1868 and 1875, had broadened into a Royal Commission on the Housing of the Working Classes, established in 1884 and reporting the following year.

In London, the implementation of the Cross Act – which allowed local authorities to purchase areas designated for slum clearance, offering the cleared sites for sale to responsible private agencies prepared to erect 'model dwellings' for at least as many people as had been displaced – had been the responsibility of the Metropolitan Board of Works (MBW). But the Board, too, was the subject of investigation for corruption and malpractice, and there were demands for its replacement; this duly came to pass during the Ripper crisis with the passage of the Local Government Act of 1888, which established the London County Council. The LCC assumed the slum clearance powers previously vested in the MBW and soon – in 1890 – acquired additional powers to build and manage council housing.

Thirdly, the Trafalgar Square riots of 1886–87 and subsequent industrial unrest were interpreted by the political establishment as a threat to the West End from an out-of-control, potentially revolutionary, East End proletariat. While the source of the problem lay in a low-wage, casual labour market, the quick-fix solution involved surveillance and the inculcation of discipline and order among the poor; and one way of achieving this was to replace the labyrinth of alleys and courts of ill-managed lodgings with more easily policed straight streets and efficiently supervised model dwellings.

All these concerns came together in autumn 1888 in public and press reactions to the Whitechapel murders. By late September 1888, the correspondence columns of the *Daily Telegraph* were occupied by a debate about 'a safe four per cent': the argument that it 'would pay capitalists and small investors to form companies to erect buildings suitable . . . for the accommodation particularly of those who are regarded

Coopers Place, Whitechapel, *c.*1900
Off the main thoroughfares of Whitechapel and Spitalfields, there were many narrow
alleyways and courts with small terraced houses and sometimes empty buildings.
The East End was often referred to as a labyrinth.

as outcasts and semi-criminal'. It was claimed that existing 'model dwellings', such as those provided by the Peabody Trust, the Improved Industrial Dwellings Company and, in the East End, the recently formed East End Dwellings Company and Four Per Cent Industrial Dwellings Company, catered mainly for respectable and regularly employed artisans, and actually made the situation worse for the poorest, including many who were deserving but unfortunate. In 1883, discussing *How the Poor Live*, George Sims lamented that

> the poor – the honest poor – have been driven by the working of the Artizans' Dwellings Acts, and the clearance of rookery after rookery, to come and herd with thieves and wantons . . . Among all the cruelties practised on the poor in the name of Metropolitan Improvements this one deserves mentioning – that the labourer earning a precarious livelihood with his wife and his children have been driven at last to accept the shelter of a thieves' kitchen.

It seemed perverse that they and the 'outcasts and semi-criminal' among whom they were forced to live were paying at least 4d. per person per night for a bed in a common lodging-house, at least 2 shillings per person per week, and twice that for a barely furnished room of their own in a multi-occupied house, when the rent of a room in a model dwelling also averaged about 2 shillings per week.

THE PROBLEM WITH MODEL DWELLINGS

Model dwellings companies were reluctant to accept the most marginal for a variety of reasons. One reason why they could charge as little as 2 shillings per room per week was that their management costs were low: tenants paid their rent on time, obeyed the rules and regulations about noise and helping to keep clean the communal areas, including toilets, laundry rooms and staircases, and remained in the same flats for relatively long periods of time, therefore saving on the costs of whitewashing and repapering that were invariably undertaken when there was a change of tenant. But the very poorest were constantly on the move to wherever casual or seasonal employment was available; or they were 'shiftless', falling in and out with partners and kin. Charles Booth, in his work on mapping the East End, referred to the constant and ultimately usually circular mobility of the poor, flitting from street to street but never very far, and George Gissing provided a brilliant fictional evocation of the process (not in Whitechapel but in the poorest parts of Clerkenwell) in his novel, *The Nether World* (1889). On Dorset Street, Spitalfields, the only names to appear in both 1881 and 1891 censuses were those of local tradesmen and their families: Barnet Price, a Jewish grocer at no. 7; Jane Brooks, a coal dealer at no. 39; Alexander McQueen, a blind mat manufacturer and lodging-house keeper at no. 28; Mary Carey, a general dealer, who had moved from no. 33 on the north side of the street to no. 8, immediately opposite; and John (Jack) and Daniel McCarthy, grocers, based at no. 27, but with property interests throughout the street. Around them, the other eight or nine hundred inhabitants of the street changed constantly.

Consider some of the Ripper's victims. Catherine Eddowes and her partner John Kelly regarded the lodging-house at no. 55 Flower and Dean Street as home, yet she had not slept there in the week preceding her murder. Returning to London on Thursday from three days' hop-picking in Kent, they spent Thursday night in the casual ward of Shoe Lane (Farringdon) Workhouse because they had no money to pay for a bed in the lodging-house. On Friday night, Kelly slept at no. 55 but Eddowes went to the casual ward of Mile End Workhouse. On Saturday Kelly heard that she had been arrested for drunkenness and locked up in Bishopsgate police station. He assumed she would be kept there overnight and released next morning, as had happened on previous occasions, so he wasn't concerned when she didn't turn up at no. 55 on Saturday night. Similarly, Elizabeth Stride was reported to have lived for about six years, on and off, in a lodging-house at no. 32 Flower and Dean Street, but for most of the two years prior to her death she lived in a lodging-house in Dorset Street with her partner, Michael Kidney. However, at intervals she had left him and wandered off. He saw her last on 25 September, five days before her murder, but from the 27th to the 29th she had been back at the Flower and Dean Street lodgings. The permanence and the discipline of model dwellings would not have suited either couple, whatever the cost.

Model dwellings also kept down maintenance costs by prohibiting tenants from using their flats as workplaces. Sims interviewed a mother and daughter in a one-room dwelling, 'about eight feet square', for which they paid 4 shillings per week in rent. He pointed out that for 4 shillings they could find much better lodgings. But respectable landlords would not tolerate the work on which the women depended – pulling rabbit-skins to remove all the loose fluff. So they were obliged to pay the extortionate rents demanded by slum landlords; and one reason the landlords could charge such rents was that slum clearance was reducing the stock of low-quality, anything-tolerated, no-questions-asked lodgings.

An average rent of 2 shillings per room in model dwellings also disguised the fact that three- and four-room flats were usually proportionally cheaper than the one-room flats that might accommodate the poorest. In the East End Dwellings Company's Lolesworth Buildings (opened in 1887), a one-room flat cost 2s. 10d. per week,[1] while in the Peabody Trust's oldest estate, erected in Commercial Street, Spitalfields, in 1863, there were seven three-room flats at 5 shillings per week, 47 two-room flats, mostly at 4 shillings per week, but only three one-room flats, priced at 2s. 6d. per week. At the Trust's Whitechapel estate, Glasshouse Street (close to St Katharine's and London Docks), one of the Cross Act estates opened in 1881, there were 42 one-room flats at 3 shillings per week, but they were still vastly outnumbered by 244 two- and

Matchbox making at home, *c.*1900
In the 1880s, matchbox making was an important yet poorly paid home trade in the East End.
The payment for each gross (twelve dozen) boxes was 2½d. Families worked from early in
the morning till late at night, sometimes even all night. Their employers provided all the
materials except the paste or glue.

three-room flats rented at between 4s. 3d. and 5s. 9d. per week. Moreover, Peabody would not allow levels of occupancy of more than two adults or one adult and two children per room. Families living in one room in a house on Dorset Street would be expected to pay for two or three rooms if they moved into model dwellings.

Model dwellings erected in Whitechapel in the late 1870s and early 1880s (and

Lolesworth Buildings rent book, 1895

Rent was collected each Tuesday by the East End Dwellings Company's agent. The rules and regulations governing the tenancy are clearly set out on the inside cover of the rent book.

also on the sites of other former 'rookeries' in Westminster, Covent Garden and Clerkenwell) relied on an indirect subsidy: the Metropolitan Board of Works compulsorily purchased slums at their full market value, cleared the sites and then offered them for sale to developers, mostly limited-dividend companies and charitable trusts, who acquired them for a fraction of their market price. Not only was this awkward to justify in the context of free-market liberalism but, practically, it provoked opposition from ratepayers who objected to their rates being used to subsidise working-class housing. This was one reason why, by the late 1880s, the Cross Act was falling into disuse and why, even among schemes that were approved, their extent was often reduced at the planning stage. A correspondent to the *Daily Telegraph* on 21 September 1888 complained: 'Why . . . did the Metropolitan Board of Works abolish the one half of Thrawl-street and of Flower and Dean-street and leave the other half still standing? Why did they stop short in pulling down a portion and not the whole of Wentworth-street? For how long will the Fashion-street scheme remain "under consideration"?' The short answer was that it was too expensive. The total cost to the Board of Works of the 'Goulston St and Flower and Dean St' scheme, even in its emasculated form, was nearly £372,000, but the receipts from selling the cleared land to a variety of tenement and model dwellings companies were less than £88,000, a net cost to the ratepayer of £284,000.

It was also feared that part of Whitechapel's problem was an excess of charity. Too many philanthropic dwellings, shelters for the homeless, soup kitchens and settlement houses positively attracted, to use the rector of Spitalfields' choice phrase, 'the human wreckage of the kingdom'. This demoralised the recipients of charity. Not only the occupiers but also the owners of slums were thought to benefit from misguided charity. The prospect of overgenerous compensation created a speculative market in slums. Unscrupulous landlords or their agents acquired slum property in anticipation of making a profit when it was compulsorily purchased by the Metropolitan Board of Works. Those who received compensation were rarely the occupiers about to be displaced, but the freeholders and leaseholders who were being deprived of their income from rents. The more tenants you could cram in, the greater your rent roll, the more compensation you could claim. Moreover, in anticipation of condemnation, it was obviously foolish to spend money on maintenance or repairs. In his play *Widowers' Houses* (1892), George Bernard Shaw implied that much of this exploitative activity contributed to the income and annuities that sustained

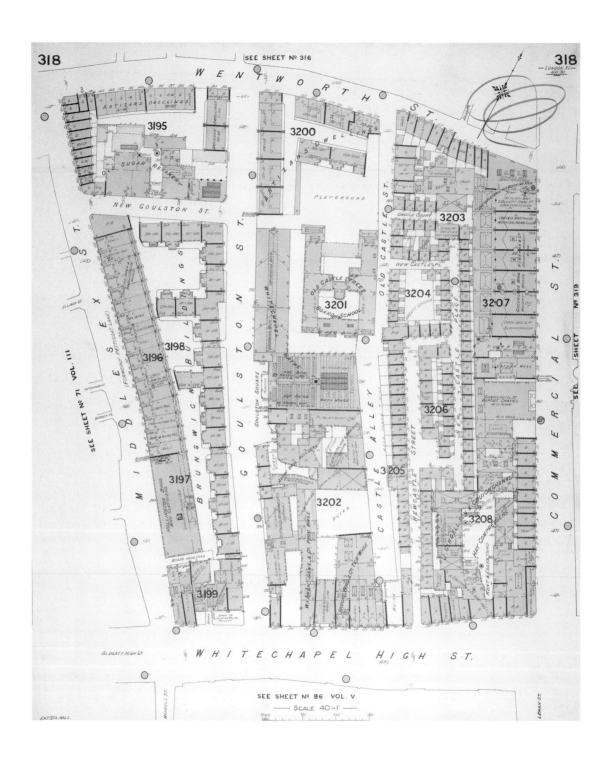

WENTWORTH ST.

3195

ARTIZANS DWELLINGS

OLD SUGAR REFINERY

3200

ARTIZANS DWELLINGS

PLAYGROUND

CASTLE COURT

3203

NEW CASTLE PL.

NEW GOULSTON ST.

3201

OLD CASTLE STREET
BOARD SCHOOL

3204

3207

S.

MIDDLESEX

BRUNSWICK BUILDINGS

(FORMERLY PETTICOAT LANE)

3196

3198

GOULSTON SQUARE

WHITECHAPEL

NEW CASTLE STREET

NEW CASTLE PLACE

3206

COMMERCIAL ST.

Nº 319

SEE SHEET

3197

HOLLINGTON BROS.

CASTLE ALLEY

3205

3202

RUINS

3208

HAY COMPRESSERS

J. INGELL & SONS
CRUIKSHANKS

KENT MESSENGER YARD

3199

WHITECHAPEL HIGH ST.
ALDGATE HIGH ST.

middle-class proprietors living in West End luxury, protected by distance and a chain of middlemen from needing to know how their wealth was generated.

When clearance eventually occurred, the new tenants of model dwellings were rarely the same people who had been displaced. Most occupiers of such blocks fell into Booth's classes D, E and F, at worst on the margins of poverty. Going back to Booth's original notebooks in the London School of Economics, Jim Yelling classified 56 per cent of tenants at Peabody's Glasshouse Street estate as in Booth's class E, 38 per cent in Class D, and only 6 per cent in Class B. In the East End Dwellings Company's Katherine Buildings just to the west, the population was poorer – 26 per cent in Class B – but Class E still made up 35 per cent of tenants. Jerry White contrasted the class structure of the newly erected Rothschild Buildings, opened in 1887 by the Four Per Cent Industrial Dwellings Company, with that of part of the Flower and Dean Street rookery which it replaced. In 1871, 78 per cent of residents could be classed as 'unskilled' or 'semi-skilled' and 17 per cent as 'skilled'. After redevelopment, 70 per cent of the inmates of Rothschild Buildings were skilled and only 9 per cent semi-skilled or unskilled. Inward-looking Peabody blocks, facing on to central courtyards and subject to the surveillance of estate superintendents and porters, ensured that tenants were as safe from the contagious immorality of the 'criminal classes' as they were from more medical forms of contagion. It was rare for displaced slum-dwellers to end up in the new model dwellings – only 11 of the 167 displaced from the last phase of clearance at Whitechapel and Limehouse moved into

꒥꒙ Goad map of the area between Wentworth Street and Whitechapel High Street, 1890
Brunswick Buildings were ranged along the western side of Goulston Street facing the
Whitechapel Baths. At the artisan dwellings at the top eastern end of the street, a portion
of Catherine Eddowes' apron was discovered along with the chalk message on the wall –
'The Juwes are the men That Will not be Blamed for nothing'.

the new Peabody dwellings and evidently they didn't stay for long; as the superintendent of the Peabody estate told Beatrice Webb, then a volunteer housing manager on the neighbouring East End Dwellings Co. estate: 'We had a rough lot to begin with, had to weed them of the old inhabitants – now only take in men with regular employment.'

In Spitalfields, the much older Peabody estate (with none of the protection of access from an internal courtyard) surprisingly accommodated proportionally fewer married or cohabiting couples than houses on Dorset Street, just the other side of Spitalfields Market, but there were other reasons for suggesting a superior class of population in the model dwellings.[2] In Dorset Street in 1891 (excluding the common lodging-houses but including houses in Miller's Court) 70 per cent of households included 'married' couples, but in Peabody Buildings the proportion was only 54 per cent. Less than a fifth of Dorset Street households were headed by women, compared to over a third in Peabody Buildings. But on Dorset Street, more than 80 per cent of households lived in one-room dwellings, whereas on the Peabody estate all but two of the 54 households occupied at least two rooms. There was an average of 1.57 persons per room in Peabody Buildings compared to 2.4 per room in houses in Miller's Court and Dorset Street; and more of the Peabody inhabitants were young children, who counted only as half-persons in official calculations that defined overcrowding as more than two persons per room. Four-fifths of Peabody residents had been born in London; on Dorset Street, fewer than two-thirds.

The difference between the two locales is accentuated when we add Dorset Street's lodging-houses into the calculation. In 1891 four lodging-houses accommodated more people than the rest of the street: there were no children in the lodging-houses save one or two who were members of the deputies' (lodging-house managers') families; two of the lodging-houses sheltered only male lodgers and in the other two men were in the majority. By contrast, there were substantially more

Commercial Street Peabody Buildings, *c.*1900

This photograph shows the triangular site of the first Peabody Buildings with shops along the ground floor. A little further along Commercial Street was the police station where many Jack the Ripper suspects were brought to be questioned. The Peabody Buildings stood opposite the Royal Cambridge Music Hall.

women than men in Peabody Buildings. Overall, Dorset Street had lots of couples, each occupying at most a single room, and lots of single men in lodging-house dormitories, but relatively few families with children, whereas Peabody Buildings had more two-generation families (even if one parent, usually the father, was absent), more older women and a much less crowded environment.

By 1890, when the total population was about 74,000, there were 23 estates of model dwellings in Whitechapel, accommodating 6,269 adults and 4,142 children in 2,790 separate flats. Yet, despite the fears of too much easy-to-get charity, and perhaps fortunately for the poorest and most marginal who only stood to lose from slum clearance and redevelopment, this was a smaller proportion than in many other parts of inner London. Whitechapel was a less attractive focus for philanthropic attention than more manageable, more easily improved slum districts further west. Neither the Peabody Trust nor the Improved Industrial Dwellings Company concentrated much of their resources on the inner East End. Peabody may have begun in Spitalfields, but their operations there were modest compared to the much larger estates which they erected in the late 1860s and 1870s in Islington, Westminster, Chelsea, Pimlico, Waterloo and Southwark. And almost the only estate where they recorded problems in attracting tenants was at Shadwell, close to the London Docks. Further west there were plenty of skilled artisans in regular employment who made for well-behaved and reliable tenants who always paid the rent on time.

The same geography was true of the Improved Industrial Dwellings Company. It built one early estate in Wapping, several modest sets of buildings in Shoreditch, Hoxton, and on Commercial Road, and a substantial estate in the then most suburban part of Bethnal Green; mostly it favoured locations further west, including areas where aristocratic landlords made sites available at minimal ground rents – in Pimlico and along the boundary between Oxford Street and Mayfair. In these localities model dwellings functioned as cordons sanitaires, protecting fashionable areas like Mayfair

Working-men's homes near Middlesex Street, c.1902

The Four Per Cent Industrial Dwellings Company was formed in 1885 to provide model tenement dwellings for Jewish families. The Charlotte de Rothschild Dwellings in Flower and Dean Street shown here opened in April 1887.

155

and Belgravia from becoming frayed at the edges and providing homes for the artisans and service workers on whom the rich relied. But in the East End there was not the same symbiotic relationship between local rich and poor, and not the same enclaves of wealth in need of protection. When George Arkell compiled statistics on 'block dwellings' for Charles Booth's poverty survey, he found that only 5.6 per cent of the population of Tower Hamlets lived in block dwellings compared to 10.9 per cent in Westminster. Moreover, the percentage who lived in *philanthropic* blocks (as opposed to generally lower-quality and more expensive speculatively built tenements) was 8.1 per cent in Westminster but just 2.1 per cent in Tower Hamlets.

WHO OWNED THE SLUMS?

Even if they were not deliberately exploitative, as Bernard Shaw implied, West End investors owned substantial chunks of the East End. For example, the Henderson family, rooted in the army, the Church of England, the Conservative Club and, geographically, in the West End, owned much of the freehold of Flower and Dean Street. Union Court and parts of Fashion Street and Brick Lane were owned by the parish of St Bride's, Fleet Street, 'let out at a mere nominal rent' of £400 per annum, but the lessee became bankrupt and the property reverted to the Capital and Counties Bank: 'being only the mortgagees, they were not under covenant to continue the improvements commenced by [the lessee]'. The *Star* (12 October 1888), which claimed the credit for 'exposing this serious scandal', noted that the appalling conditions of 'vice

A small doss-house, c.1902

The slang term for a common lodging-house was 'doss-house'. Jack London described small privately run ones as 'unmitigated horrors'. Thieving was rife in such places with occupants clasping their clothes and shoes while they slept.

157

and filth' were attributable to 'the bad way in which they let the property, and the conditions in their leases [which] made it impossible to get good tenants'. Another court was 'rented of the freeholders by two policemen, and they get a good thing out of it'. St Bride's could do nothing until the lease expired, three years hence.

That there was a market in East End property is evident from advertisements in *The Times* which can be linked to land tax records for the parish of Christ Church, Spitalfields, recording names of 'proprietors' and 'occupiers' at different dates throughout the nineteenth century. But these advertisements also indicate that property transactions were as often a consequence of death and the subsequent disposal of the deceased's estate by executors as they were speculative. In April 1876, the freehold estate of Robert Arnold, deceased, comprising nos 14 and 15 Dorset Street (and associated stabling) and nos 9, 10 and 20 Church Street, was auctioned. One Church Street house was leased, the other two and the stables were let to yearly tenants, but the two Dorset Street houses were let to weekly tenants (usually a sign of lower status). The advertisement implied that it would be easy to raise 'the present low rentals' on the short-tenancy houses. The two houses on the south side of Dorset Street, assessed at an annual rental value of £94 in the 1880s, were sold for £1,310, equivalent to fourteen years' purchase.[3] By the mid-1880s they were owned by Lewis A. White, who also owned houses in Freeman Street, Tenter Street and Bell Lane, but 'occupied' by William Crossingham who ran them as lodgings (housing 57 persons in 11 households in 1881). Crossingham lived next door, at 16–20 Dorset Street, which he and his wife ran as a common lodging-house (164 male lodgers in 1881). By 1890 he was also running a new lodging-house at no. 35, further west and on the north side of the street, a site recorded as 'pulled down' in the 1881 census and as 'land' in the 1886 tax assessment but which accommodated 72 lodgers (36 of each sex) in 1891. Annie Chapman had been a lodger at 35 Dorset Street for four months prior to her death and spent her last evening sitting in the kitchen (though she had not slept there during

Dorset Street, c. 1888 Principal Property Owners and leaseholders

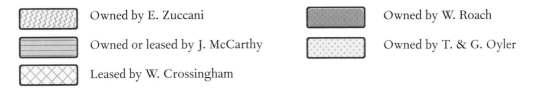

Owned by E. Zuccani

Owned or leased by J. McCarthy

Leased by W. Crossingham

Owned by W. Roach

Owned by T. & G. Oyler

the week preceding her murder, and was obliged to go out on the street before 2 a.m. 'because she had not 4d to pay for her bed'). Crossingham was still reported as owning 'considerable property in Dorset Street', including two lodging-houses, in 1901.

Numbers 37, 38 and 39 Dorset Street, described as 'three freehold eight-roomed houses and shops', let to weekly tenants and producing an income of £156 per annum, were advertised for sale in February 1877. Evidently they did not attract a buyer, for they were re-advertised in December, when they sold for £1,555 (i.e. 10 years' purchase, although if the assessed value of £105 is used, this becomes 15 years' purchase). By 1886, if not before, they were part of Jack McCarthy's property empire, accommodating (in 1891) 15 households in one room each and two households who each had the luxury of two rooms, a grand total of 46 inhabitants.

Numbers 26 and 27 Dorset Street, 'two freehold houses and shops', along with 'six small houses, forming Miller's-court, in rear', together let at £202 16s. per annum, were offered at auction in September 1881. In the land tax for 1872–73, the proprietor was listed as A. Barnett, and in 1886 and 1889 as M. Barnett (which suggests that the properties failed to sell in 1881). In each year, the 'occupiers' were recorded as 'tenants', i.e. weekly, monthly or at most yearly tenants, not sufficiently long term to be designated as individually named 'lessees'. In practice, we know that McCarthy was the resident occupier of no. 27 in both 1881 and 1891, and landlord of the two-room (one-up, one-down) houses in Miller's Court which, by 1891, were let out as one-room dwellings. Mary Kelly was murdered on 9 November 1888 in a room at the rear of no. 26, opening on to Miller's Court. In evidence at the inquest, McCarthy attested that Kelly's rent was 4s. 6d. per week, but that she was 29 shillings in arrears at the time of her death. The rent of 4s. 6d. per room per week approximates quite closely to £202 16s. per annum, but it has been a subject of much speculation how (and why) McCarthy could condone arrears equivalent to nearly seven weeks' rent. In model dwellings, rent arrears were rarely allowed, but in more conventional working-class housing where tenants had temporarily fallen on hard times, a landlord might judge it cheaper to allow them to remain, especially if their difficulties were part of a wider trade recession making it impossible to recruit new tenants without reducing the rent or spending money making the property more attractive. But in properties such as those on Dorset Street where there was a very rapid turnover of occupants, McCarthy's behaviour seems strange (though apparently unquestioned at the time). In contrast to 37–39 Dorset Street, where an advertised (gross) annual rental of £156 can be set alongside an assessed (net) value of £105 (i.e. about a third of gross rents went on repairs, maintenance, rent collection and an allowance for bad debts), the difference between McCarthy's rental income (£202 16s.) and assessment (£72, made up of two front houses worth £20 and £22, and six Miller's Court houses each valued at £5) was huge. Either it was assumed that management costs and repairs would take a substantial proportion of gross rents or McCarthy was charging massively inflated rents, which is perhaps why he could afford to be so generous over arrears.

McCarthy was also the 'occupier' of two houses in Great Pearl Street, which he ran as common lodging-houses. Research by Fiona Rule reveals that by the 1910s McCarthy owned the freeholds of nos 2, 4, 8, 11, 12, 26, 27, 28, 29, 30, 37, 38 and 39, several of which he had first leased for several years before purchasing the freehold, as well as the leasehold of no. 3 Dorset Street.[4] He also ran two lodging-houses in Limehouse and another Spitalfields lodging-house, on Lower Keate Street at the heart of the Flower and Dean Street rookery. In addition, by the 1910s he owned the freeholds of nos 21, 22, 26 and 27 White's Row, perhaps unsurprisingly since properties on the south side of Dorset Street backed on to the north side of White's Row. Several other freeholders of Dorset Street houses also owned property on White's Row to the south or on Brushfield Street to the north. This spatial pattern is significant because it indicates the layout of property in Spitalfields: a labyrinth where not only marked passages and alleys but also routes through private property allowed movement between streets.

As a 'local' landlord, McCarthy appears quite typical. For example, the lodging-house at 34 Flower and Dean Street was owned by Alfred Coates, who kept a chandler's shop at 36 Dorset Street although he lived in Whitecross Street, on the northern edge of the City, another rookery undergoing redevelopment. Mrs Wilmot, the proprietor of one lodging-house in George Yard, also ran two more in Wentworth Street, and lived in Brick Lane where she was in business as a baker; Thomas and George Oyler, who owned 9–10 Dorset Street, a huge men's common lodging-house known as Edinburgh Chambers (197 inmates in 1881, 180 in 1891), appeared in the *Post Office Directory* as lodging-house keepers of 106–7 St George Street, East and St James' Chambers, Poplar High Street, and bakers, 201 Poplar High Street.

Concluding the history of *Times* advertisements for Dorset Street property, in May 1889 the executors of the estate of Robert Wagstaff offered for sale freehold houses on Brushfield Street, Church Street and Princes Street plus the long leaseholds of nos 28 and 29 Dorset Street. The freehold was owned by E. Zuccani, who also owned houses, a beerhouse and a factory on Brushfield Street and Hanbury Street. Seven years later, the freeholds of 28 and 29 Dorset Street, along with nos 31 and 32 (the Blue Coat Boy public house, previously owned by H. Todd), came on the market, again as the result of trustees winding up an estate that also included property in Lincoln's Inn, Upper Thames Street and Deptford, another example of an estate that incorporated East End lodging-houses in the same portfolio as City, West End and suburban investments.[5]

FOR AND AGAINST LODGING-HOUSES

Even the most ardent housing reformers acknowledged that the poor had to live somewhere. It was no good simply demolishing slums or closing down lodging-houses deemed to be immoral. Lord Shaftesbury's Common Lodging-houses Act (1851) and the 1866 Sanitary Act variously legislated to ensure that lodging-houses were

'Singles' and 'doubles' in a common lodging-house, Spitalfields, 1886

*In some lodging-houses the blankets were marked with the words 'STOLEN' and the name of
the proprietor. It was noted that this 'arrangement prevents pawning, but does not always prevent
the feminine lodger from making them into useful under-clothing during the night, the only
drawback to this being the large letters sprawling over the garments.'*

regulated and inspected, but the focus was entirely on their physical, sanitary condition. Lodging-house keepers were required 'to register their names and addresses,
to give the police inspector appointed for the duty free access at all times, to cleanse
the premises, to limewash the walls and ceilings twice a year, and to give immediate
notice of an outbreak of infectious disease'. The latter was duly noted by the Medical
Officer of Health in his quarterly reports. In the last quarter of 1881, for example,
four inmates of the lodging-house at 30 Dorset Street were admitted to Whitechapel
Infirmary suffering from typhus while, in the mid-1890s, the numbers of infirmary

admissions from some lodging-houses, presumably for less serious diseases, annually ran into the hundreds.

Admissions to Whitechapel Infirmary from selected common lodging-houses

Address	1895	1896	1897
41 Commercial Street	246	252	234
9 Dorset Street	75	80	62
11 Dorset Street	16	11	15
17 Dorset Street	104	99	101
30 Dorset Street		51	58
35 Dorset Street		17	16
56 Flower and Dean Street	30	28	39
58 Flower and Dean Street	65	53	68
4 Paternoster Row	39	38	32
77 Whitechapel Road	239	224	250

Source: *Annual Reports on Sanitary Conditions of the Whitechapel District for 1895–97*

Lodging-house keepers were required to provide 300 cubic feet per bed (less than 7 ft x 5 ft x 9 ft, which indicates how little space was required around each bed). But, as countless reporters and correspondents observed, little regard was paid to the *moral* condition of lodging-houses. 'One who knows' informed *Times* readers about 'whole rows of so-called "registered" lodging-houses' in Dorset Street, Flower and Dean Street and Thrawl Street, 'each of which is practically a brothel and a focus of crime'. He urged the 'suppression of these haunts of crime and the dispersion of their lawless population', but other correspondents recognised the inadequacy of this response: 'There are no lower streets in London, and if they are driven out of these, to what streets are they to go? . . . If she [writing of women like Annie Chapman] is systematically "dispersed", two results will follow. She will carry her taint to streets hitherto untainted. And she herself will be mulcted in larger sums than before for the accommodation.'

A succession of middle-class social explorers reported back on their visits to lodging-houses. Some romanticised their experiences, portraying the residents, and especially the communal 'kitchens', in reassuringly picturesque language: 'At a little table in the corner of the room are seated men and women, roughly merry over their midday meal, while in friendly

Outside a lodging-house, Flower and Dean Street, Spitalfields, c.1900

argument the inevitable can of beer circulates quickly among another group. Here is a woman busily preparing her wares from out her scanty stock of many-coloured tissues' reported the *Leytonstone Express and Independent*. The *Evening News*' 'special correspondent' visited 55 Flower and Dean Street, Catherine Eddowes' lodging-house, and reported on the 'capacious kitchen filled with men, women and children of all ages, and redolent with the fumes of cooked dishes and boiling tea'. As the hours passed, so 'the proceedings in the kitchen became more lively. There was very little drunkenness visible . . . Girls commenced singing songs, and the "poet of the company" entertained the room with quotations from Shakespeare and from his own composition, the latter bearing chiefly upon the horrible murder of the day.' *Dickens' Dictionary of London* (1879) provided a glowing description of the effects of the Common Lodging-house Act, noting 'the comparative sweetness of these dormitories, even when crowded with tramps and thieves of the lowest class'. Even Charles Booth acknowledged that 'registered lodging-houses . . . mark a great improvement. However bad their inmates may be, these houses undoubtedly represent the principles of order, cleanliness, and decency.'

The trouble with lodging-houses lay both in the character of their environs and in the forced intimacy between inmates which periodically erupted into violence or offered opportunities for premeditated assault. Middle-class visitors who romanticised community life inside lodging-houses nevertheless remained terrified of having to walk along the street outside. The streets were never empty, except perhaps in the mornings when they *ought* to have been busy with work, but they were populated by a threatening, dangerous class. J. Ewing Ritchie (1880) took his readers for a walk down Flower and Dean Street: 'your presence is not welcomed in the street. You are not a lodger, that is clear. Curious and angry eyes follow you all the way. Of course your presence there – the appearance of anything respectable – is an event which creates alarm rather than surprise.' Richard Rowe's (1881) account was more orientalist, referring to his policeman-guide as a 'dragoman' who ensured he was not assaulted or robbed during his passage down the street. Hugh Edward Hoare ran an East End lodging-house for just under two years, 1886–88, as a form of social experiment: 'I had only twice walked through the street, and the first time I was warned by a policeman, as I turned down into it, to look out where I was going to, and the second time I was advised by a man, as I was leaving it, not to come there again.' Over four consecutive Saturday nights, between midnight and 1 a.m., his manager observed 12 robberies in the street outside their lodging-house.[6]

The kitchen of a common lodging-house, Spitalfields, 1886
The lodgers cooked their own meals but the landlord owned the utensils such as
the teapots, frying-pans and saucepans.

Grudges against lodging-house keepers, quarrels among lodgers, and quarrels over women were matched by robberies in the limited privacy of a lodging-house cubicle. Daniel Shea violently attacked Fanny Markham, wife of a Dorset Street lodging-house keeper, late one Sunday evening. PC Doughty found Shea in the lodging-house kitchen, where he resisted arrest and had to be held down until the arrival of another constable. Mr Markham claimed that some men had paid Shea to come to the house and create a disturbance. Jeremiah Mahoney and Richard Atkins quarrelled at their lodging-house at 30 Dorset Street. When the latter returned two

Kitchen in a single women's lodging-house, Spitalfields, *c.*1900
Lodging-house kitchens were the centre of communal life.

hours later, the former 'suddenly snatched up a heavy iron spade, used at the fire-place, and struck [him] a fearful blow across the face with the edge of the iron of the spade', nearly cutting off his nose. On Boxing Day 1888, Patrick Manning travelled by cab to a Dorset Street lodging-house where a woman he knew lodged. When he entered her room, accompanied by the cabman, another lodger tried to enter the room but was shut out 'after a struggle'. When Manning and the cabman left, the lodger attacked them on the stairs, stabbing Manning in the thigh. A quarrel between two female lodgers in a Dorset Street lodging-house culminated in one stabbing the other in the face with a pair of scissors.[7] Annie Chapman had bruises on her temple and

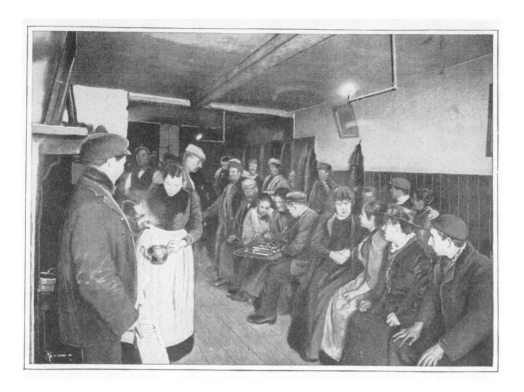

Kitchen in a common lodging-house, Spitalfields, *c.*1900
Those without regular employment would sit in the kitchen, keeping warm next to the fire,
chatting and passing the time of day.

chest, caused by a fight with another lodging-house inmate over the loan of a piece of soap only a few days before her murder.

In October 1888, Mary McCarthy, a lodger, was convicted of stabbing Ann Neason, deputy of a lodging-house in George Yard, in the face and neck with a skewer. McCarthy was 'well-known' at the police court, and evidently well known at the lodging-house, where the owner, Mrs Wilmot, had told the deputy to refuse her entry. The following week, Mary Hawkes, 18, and James Fordham, 21, were charged with assaulting a Scandinavian student who – in a supposedly intoxicated state – agreed to go with Hawkes to a common lodging-house at 34 Flower and Dean Street, where he paid 8d. for a 'double'. Fordham arrived soon afterwards and paid 4d. for a single. PC Dennis heard the student cry for help, and arrived to see him thrown downstairs minus his purse and trousers. The deputy remembered admitting Hawkes and the student, but 'could not account for Fordham being afterwards found with Mary Hawkes in a "double", when he paid for a single bed'. As Dennis explained, although the double beds were partitioned off, the partitions reached neither to the floor nor the ceiling: 'A person might pass from one to another room by a good squeeze.'[8]

FURNISHED ROOMS

There were similar cases in what sound more like 'furnished rooms' than lodging-houses. James Fairey, 17, cabin-boy, claimed to have been robbed of £21 by Elizabeth Spurden, James Wilson and others, in a 'low house' in Dorset Street. He said he had just arrived in port after 'a very long voyage' and had received the money as wages. He 'fell in with' Spurden, 'who took him home, saying she would provide him with a dinner'. When she and her friends discovered he had money, 'they seized him by the arms and legs, and held him while they rifled his pockets'. But it subsequently transpired that Fairey himself had stolen the money, which his master kept 'under a sofa in the state room of the ship'. Henry Sutton, an agricultural labourer from Chadwell Heath, met Annie Williams in a public house in Whitechapel, where she invited him home to supper in a house in Dorset Street: here four men immediately 'rushed into the room, and . . . demanded what he was doing there . . . The men knelt upon his chest, and held his limbs, whilst one of the gang cut the pockets out of his trousers, and obtained all the money he had about him.'[9]

In fact, many commentators claimed that 'furnished rooms' were far worse than common lodging-houses because they were not subject to the same regulation and inspection. The press regularly reported deaths attributable to the unhealthy living

Neath Place, *c.*1900
Photograph by John Galt.

conditions in such rooms. Robert Lynn, 58, paid 2 shillings per week for a room in 38 Dorset Street, 'which was not fit to live in, as, in addition to the offensive smell from the stables over which it was immediately situated, it was very dark'. His death was

171

attributed to 'gangrene of the lungs, accelerated by the poisonous atmosphere in which deceased lived'. At 4 Dorset Street, the Freedman family (parents and four children) paid 4s. 6d. for two rooms. Mr Freedman 'did not earn 10s a week'. His wife agreed to nurse a baby for 6 shillings per week, but the woman who gave her the baby disappeared without paying anything. The baby died, in the words of the inquest jury's verdict, 'from inflammation of the lungs, accelerated by want of proper food and nourishment, which was brought about by the impoverished condition of the Freedmans'.[10]

PROMISCUOUS SPACES

In lodging-houses there was virtually no privacy, yet many inmates developed an attachment to a particular lodging-house which they regarded as home, even if they did not sleep there on a permanent basis. Howard J. Goldsmid explained in his *Dottings of a Dosser* (1886):

> When you enter the 'kitchen' of a 'doss-'ouse', it would be a mistake to suppose that all the people you meet there are going to spend the night under its roof. Many of them are 'reg'lar 'uns', who, in consideration of their constant patronage are permitted to spend the evening, or a portion of it, before the blazing coke fire, for though the deputy will give no trust, he knows better than to offend a regular lodger. As the evening wears on, however, these poor wretches become restless and moody. They pace the floor with their hands in their otherwise empty pockets, glancing towards the door at each fresh arrival to see if a 'pal' has come in from whom it may be possible to borrow the halfpence necessary to complete their doss-money. At last, their final hope being gone, they shuffle out into the streets and prepare to spend the night with only the sky for a canopy.

Frying Pan Alley, *c*.1900

At any sign of a disturbance in the small streets and alleys of Spitalfields and Whitechapel, a crowd would gather to watch. Jack London in his book, People of the Abyss, *sets out to visit a 'sweated' one-room shoemaker's workshop in Frying Pan Alley, north of Middlesex Street. Outside he finds a 'spawn of children cluttered the slimy pavement, for all the world like tadpoles just turned frogs on the bottom of a dry pond. In a narrow doorway, so narrow that perforce we stepped over her, sat a woman with a young babe, nursing at breasts grossly naked and libelling all the sacredness of motherhood.'*

This was the situation that faced Annie Chapman, who spent most of the evening before her death in the kitchen of 35 Dorset Street. When Timothy Donovan, the deputy, at last asked her for her lodging money: 'She said, "I have not got it. I am weak and ill and have been in the Infirmary." Donovan told her she knew the rules, when she went out to get some money.'

Chapman's body was found between four and five hours later in the yard at the back of 29 Hanbury Street, a classic example of a house divided into 'furnished rooms'. Here, there may have been private space for the occupants in their own rooms, but nobody claimed responsibility for the common parts – the hallway, passageways, stairs and back yard. The front door to 29 Hanbury Street was never locked and usually open, allowing access to the stairs and yard, which were occasionally used by prostitutes as places to take clients or by the homeless trying to avoid spending the night 'with only the sky for a canopy'. As a matter of course, cries for help would be ignored, excluded from residents' consciousness along with any other extraneous noise. In *How the Poor Live* (1883) George Sims had reported on a visit to a widow and her six children:

> Her wretched apartment was on the street level, and behind it was the common yard of the tenement. In this yard the previous night a drunken sailor had been desperately maltreated and left for dead. I asked the woman if she had not heard the noise, and why she didn't interfere. 'Heard it?' was the reply; 'well, we ain't deaf, but they're a rum lot in this here house, and we're used to rows. There ain't a night passes as there ain't a fight in the passage or a drunken row; but why should I interfere? Tain't no business of mine.'

Elizabeth Prater, who occupied the room above Mary Kelly's in Miller's Court, claimed that at about 4 a.m. she 'distinctly heard in a low tone and in a woman's voice a cry of "Oh! Murder".' But she ignored it 'as they were continually hearing cries of murder in the court'.

At 29 Hanbury Street, 'a fair example of a large number of houses in the neighbourhood', built for Spitalfields weavers and then converted into dwellings for the poor, 17 persons occupied the house. Two rooms on the ground floor were occupied

Back yard and rows of houses, *c.*1900
At the inquest report into Annie Chapman's murder the doors, passages and yard at
29 Hanbury Street were described in detail. Multiple occupancy made it difficult to establish
who might have used the common spaces of the building.

by Mrs Annie Hardman, who used the front parlour as a cat's meat shop, but also as a bedroom for herself and her son. Amelia Richardson, widow, used the ground-floor back room for cooking but slept, with her 14-year-old grandson, in the first-floor front room. The first-floor back was tenanted by the 'weak-minded' but 'inoffensive' Alfred Walker and his father. Mr Thompson, carman, his wife and adopted little girl

175

occupied the second-floor front. Mr and Mrs Copsey, cigar-makers, occupied the second-floor back. John Davis, carman, shared the third-floor (attic) front room with his wife and three sons; and the elderly Sarah Cox occupied the third-floor back. People were coming and going at all hours, and one or two claimed to have heard the odd noise or shout, but nothing that seemed worth their attention. Mrs Richardson acknowledged that 'People frequently went through into the back yard, and perhaps some who had no business there'. Her son, who did not live there but worked as a porter in Spitalfields Market, 'had been to the house and in the passage at all hours of the night and had seen lots of strangers there. These he had seen at all hours. He had seen both men and women there, and had turned them out.' Yet nothing had ever been stolen from the house except for some tools in the cellar. This 'promiscuous' use of space ran completely contrary to a middle-class defence of private space. It is no surprise that one of the indicators of low status used by George Duckworth in his perambulations with police officers, updating Charles Booth's poverty maps in 1897–99, was 'open doors'.

There were 'furnished rooms' and common lodging-houses all over London, so we cannot simply 'explain' the social conditions of the East End, let alone the Whitechapel murders, as resulting from the system of housing provision. Nevertheless, the concentration of 'low' lodgings was extreme in parts of Spitalfields and Whitechapel. The report of the Metropolitan Police Chief Commissioner recorded exactly 1,000 registered common lodging-houses in London in 1889, providing accommodation for 31,651 persons. By far the greatest concentration – about 150 lodging-houses accommodating more than 6,000 lodgers – was to be found within the limits of Middlesex Street to the west, Baker's Row to the east and Whitechapel Road to the south. There were 1,150 lodging-house beds in Flower and Dean Street, and nearly 700 in Dorset Street. Across London, some registered lodgings were hostels for the lower middle class and others were run by philanthropic agencies; in Spitalfields these included the Providence Row Night Refuge on Crispin Street, facing the western end of Dorset Street, established in 1868, and offering 302 beds to men, women and children,[11] and the Victoria Home, established by Lord Radstock, in a warehouse in Commercial Street, which had space for 500. However, the vast majority were 4d. a bed doss-houses.

WHAT HAPPENED NEXT?

What were the consequences of the Ripper murders for East End housing? Almost immediately, a demand for more regulation, more slum clearance, more public exposure of slum landlords. As early as September 1888, Canon Barnett, the Warden of Toynbee Hall, wrote to *The Times* proposing, among other things, 'the control of tenement houses by responsible landlords'. Writing in the wake of further violent crime on the streets of Whitechapel in 1894, Barnett observed that 'The murders of a few years ago roused reforming energy, and created a public opinion strong enough to compel the West London landlords of the houses in which vice and crime were nourished to use their powers to clear out their tenants.' Certainly, some discomforted ground landlords, such as the Henderson family, offered parts of their estate for sale as leases and sub-leases fell in. The beneficiaries were the East End Dwellings Company, the Four Per Cent Industrial Dwellings Company and the prolific private developer, Abraham Davis: all of these erected tenement blocks and rows of shops with flats during the 1890s. By 1900, there were 3,748 model dwelling apartments in Whitechapel, for 15,494 inhabitants. The number of common lodging-houses correspondingly declined: from 149 in 1889, to 141 in 1890, 101 in 1892 (though the number in Dorset Street actually increased slightly while those on Flower and Dean Street were almost totally wiped out), 86 in 1894, and 73 in 1897.[12] By the end of the century the LCC had erected council flats on some East End sites that the

Board of Works had failed to sell to philanthropic or private developers and, more importantly, had embarked on its own housing schemes, most notably at Boundary Street, just to the north of Spitalfields.

There were also more night shelters: William Booth had already opened the first Salvation Army hostel in a West India Dock Road warehouse in February 1888, charging only a penny a night (and stimulating accusations that he was attracting more paupers into the area, who subsequently became a charge on the local rate-payers). Dr Barnardo converted two houses – on Flower and Dean Street and Dock Street, Stepney – into common lodging-houses for children (and their mothers), also charging only a penny a night.

Yet none of this went to the roots of the problem. Canon Barnett pleaded for an arousal of public opinion to 'first, compel the publication of the names of ground land-lords . . . and, secondly, compel the authorities to break up these haunts of vice'. Ten years on from the events of 1888, Barnett wrote to *The Times* again, in the wake of yet another 'horror' in Dorset Street 'which has remained unchanged in character during the whole ten years'. In fact, things were getting worse: 'more evidence of degradation and destitution, a more open flaunting of vice, and a more frequent exposure of wretchedness'. George Duckworth, Charles Booth's assistant, was more specific:

> Into Dorset St., black in map, still black – the worst street I have seen so far, thieves, prostitutes, bullies, all common lodging-houses. Some called 'doubles' with double beds for married couples, but merely another name for brothels: women, draggled, torn skirts, dirty, unkempt.

And, reporting on a talk with Inspector Miller of Hunter Street police station:

> He spoke of Dorset Street as in his opinion the worst street – in respect of poverty, misery, vice – of the whole of London. A cesspool into which had

sunk the foulest and most degraded . . . Dorset Street might be stirred but its filth would always sink again in the same spot.

The *Daily Mail* (16 July 1901) picked the same epithet – 'The Worst Street in London' – emphasising 'the cancer of the "doss house"' where 'respectable people, whose main offence is their poverty, are thrown in close and constant contact with the agents of crime', and the even worse evil of 'furnished rooms':

> You take seven or eight-roomed houses at a rent of 10s. or 11s. a week, you place on each door a padlock, and in each room you put a minimum amount of the oldest furniture to be found in the worst second-hand dealers in the slums . . . Then you let the rooms out to any comers for 10d. or 1s. a night. No questions asked.

Dorset Street had changed its name (to Duval Street), but not until 1914 were the houses in Miller's Court condemned and closed.

CHAPTER FIVE

'DEEDS OF HEROISM': WHITECHAPEL'S LADIES

ELLEN ROSS

In the autumn of 1888, the people of Whitechapel and Spitalfields – known variously as 'murderland', a 'plague spot', or 'the evil quarter-mile' – were afraid to leave their homes. Once the naphtha lamps of the shops and market stalls were extinguished and taken down, the population rushed indoors; women in particular were under a form of house arrest. Local merchants predicted their own 'utter ruin'. The only commodities selling briskly were locks; Hanbury Street lodging-houses sported brand-new ones and their tenants new keys. It was useless for Toynbee Hall's superintendent Samuel Barnett, his fellow clergymen and the local newspapers to argue that their district was as safe as any in London.[1] Prostitutes were, of course, 'thoroughly frightened' and efforts were made to help those who wanted to leave the

Factory girls, *c.*1905

The East End was a major manufacturing centre that provided employment for a growing number of women and girls. Standing outside a 'hot joint shop', or eating-house, some factory girls were probably on their lunch break. The abbreviations on the windows stood for two friendly societies, the Ancient Order of Foresters and the Ancient Order of Druids, and the third for the London Carmen's Trade Union.

181

danger zone. London city missionaries aided dozens of vulnerable prostitutes in Spitalfields, sending them to rescue homes; new night refuges were hastily organised; Salvation Army prayer meetings offered both eternal life and safety from predators as well as eternal life. Several vigilance committees (working men, shop owners, Toynbee settlers) attempted to trap the killer and protect his potential victims.[2]

Among these rescuers was a group of ladylike Sisters from the nearby East End (Methodist) Mission which had its headquarters in Cable Street, St-George's-in-the-East. They trudged in and out of the Flower and Dean and Hanbury Street 'wilderness' attempting, in spite of many changes of name and residence, to track down the prostitutes they had befriended. Some Sisters stopped on the way to sing hymns at the sites of the murders. It was their 'infinite pity for their sinful sisters which makes them careless alike of labour and danger', reported the *Methodist Recorder*. The only protection they required were the prayers of their Mission's superintendent, the Reverend Peter Thompson. One 'heroic sister' managed, at the dangerous hour of 10.30, to spirit away a 'rescued sinner', the paper reported, a woman 'whose story if it would be fully told as it was told to us, would break hearts of stone'. She was sheltered for the night and then sent by train to a distant suburb where a Mission woman would give her safe haven. The Sisters also confronted a rather fierce and dangerous pimp. While they talked with one of the prostitutes, 'a man appeared upon the scene – a reckless, atheistic, and most terrible specimen of East-end brutality. The fellow bolted the door upon the company, and then with silent prayer to God one of the ladies did battle with him and worsted him with words of prayer, and for the time being won influence over the unhappy women.' As the journalist saw it, the heroism of the churchwomen 'would astound the Christian public'.[3]

Astonishment at these scenes of female daring is unnecessary. In this and in the many more cases of religious or philanthropic women's confrontations with dangerous slum figures or locations, their heroism certainly came from relationships

Outside the London Hospital, Whitechapel Road, *c.*1900

Margaret Harkness in her novel In Darkest London *(1889) described Whitechapel Road as*
'the most cosmopolitan place in London' where 'one sees all nationalities . . . An Algerian
merchant walks arm-in-arm with a native of Calcutta. A little Italian plays pitch-and-toss with
a small Russian. A Polish Jew enjoys sauer-kraut with a German Gentile.'

with the people involved and knowledge of the district in general – knowledge gained
through practical experience and from a familiarity sometimes extending over years.

The presence in Whitechapel of a population of 'ladies' (a term used in that era without irony) from well-off districts far to the west, though not usually connected with the Ripper story, needs to be recognised. None was a victim, though Bernard Shaw did claim that if a 'duchess' had been attacked, a large reward for finding the killer would have been offered immediately. Apart from the rescuing Sisters, few of the ladies took much interest in the crimes themselves. But genteel women could be found, in hundreds or even thousands, mainly by day, in considerable numbers on the Ripper's turf during the autumn months of 1888 and indeed throughout the 1880s and 1890s. They are a reminder that Whitechapel, along with considerable portions of east London, included not only areas of the deepest poverty but also 'mixed', 'fairly comfortable' and 'middle-class' districts, according to Charles Booth's classification; that chrysanthemum displays, dog shows, school trips, Toynbee Hall classes, and other manifestations of normal life were continuing there even when the region was considered 'a hot bed of hell' by the rest of the world.[4]

Probably the largest proportion of 'slummers' (another term used by contemporaries) were women who, like the East End Mission Sisters, were volunteers with the district's enormous numbers of religious bodies, engaged in visiting local parishioners, running Sunday schools and children's clubs, singing or playing music at services and informal entertainments, even doing clerical work. There were journalists like Margaret Harkness, a novelist as well, gathering material for her articles on London's poor for the *British Weekly*. Annie Besant, socialist firebrand, was campaigning for municipal office, preparing for a November election. Margot Tennant was enlightening factory workers during their dinner hour, while Clementina Black, advocate for working women, was (more helpfully) lecturing on unionisation for women workers. Beatrice Potter (later Webb) was one of eight 'lady rent collectors' at work in the district. Eleanor Marx had explored the area earlier in 1888 and was to be a regular visitor in the years that followed.

Each of these slumming ladies working in Whitechapel had an agenda to

184

An evicted match-box maker, Bethnal Green, *c.*1900
A mother, with her two children, stands alongside all her worldly possessions – two chairs,
a wooden board, a sack of belongings and an oil-lamp.

refashion herself through her new environment, through service, or through
social reform. Did they, or their male counterparts, actually do the 'good' that they
intended? Historians have debated that question for decades. Some have emphasised
the desire of the slum visitors or the organisations they represented to control,
domesticate or tame the wild denizens of the slums. Others have, instead, focused on

Illustration from the *Illustrated Police News*, 22 September 1888
Women prepare to defend themselves as they walk the streets of Whitechapel and Spitalfields.
They brandish a stick, a knife and even a revolver.

voluntary organisations' tangible material help in providing emergency food and medical or nursing care, or on the volunteers' classes and clubs for slum children – particularly sought out by the more ambitious, upwardly mobile young people. The accomplishments of those who were social reformers or investigators in this generation have also been debated. Probably the answer is a mixture: of officious and ill-informed meddling, and real generosity, useful service and lasting change; help to some, annoyance or actual harm to others.

Local clergymen nervously anticipated that the Whitechapel crimes would frighten 'their' ladies away, leaving no one to 'cheer the leisure of their poorer brethren', the clergy being 'left to fumble at their own Gordian knots with their clumsy fingers'. But Peter Thompson boasted in early October that his stock of volunteers was actually expanding. He said impressively: 'Our women have taken their stand on almost the very flag-stones which were stained with the victims' blood, and have sung praises to God before a crowd of miserable outcasts.' Thompson's new concern, in the words of the *Methodist Recorder*, was how to 'restrain Christian women from deeds of heroism which even he, with all his enthusiasm, regards as bordering on sanctified madness'.[5]

In fact, the prestige and presumed virtue of upper-class women figured in a number of proposals – beyond rescue work – to solve the crime or protect the potential victims. Feminist activist Frances Power Cobbe advanced a corps of women detectives, guided by 'mother wit', and thus likely to be more effective than Scotland Yard. And the bungling of the police at all levels may have encouraged the literary creation of some of the first female detectives. A male vigilance committee member proposed to send in 'a body of matrons from the West End of London of all classes – the higher the better' to collaborate with a similar east London body to 'take common counsel for the relief of their erring sisters'. And there was Toynbee Hall's Henrietta Barnett's petition asking for the personal intervention of the Queen herself, with 4,000 local women's signatures. It urged the closing down of 'bad houses within whose walls such wickedness is done' and regretted the 'sad and degraded lives' of so many of 'our sisters', as uncovered in the inquests.[6]

For some decades Whitechapel had been a destination for genteel people seeking adventure, or at least a racy evening. As the extent and realities of poverty, however, became better known in the 1880s and the poor themselves more politically assertive, a 'consciousness of sin' gripped well-informed young people of the propertied classes, many of whom joined Whitechapel's dense network of philanthropic and religious ventures. The Jewish Board of Guardians, for example, founded in 1859, provided aid to the sick and to mothers giving birth, and its Ladies' Conjoint Visiting

Salvation Army women's night refuge, possibly Hanbury Street, *c.*1890

These photographs were probably taken to draw attention to the unfortunate homeless women, both young and old, and their children that sought a night refuge from the East End streets. Such images were used to show the work of the Salvation Army and help raise funds from the public. One's attention is drawn especially to the women's faces, lined and furrowed, carrying the marks of their poverty and plight. A Methodist Mission tract describes a scene in a refuge: 'There the people sit, wearing worn out boots and ragged clothing; careworn, crushed, drowsy, prematurely old; some looking low and brutal . . . Sin has marred their faces and spoilt their characters, yet many of them give fixed attention to what is said.'

On 22 May 1884, the first women's refuge in Whitechapel opened at 212 Hanbury Street. By 1889, a derelict swimming pool had been converted nearby, at 194 Hanbury Street, into a shelter for 250 women and 50 children. The refuge was managed by Captain and Mrs Ward. It was reported, not long after it opened, that one of the 'unfortunates' called out in the middle of the night, 'Lasses, I know who've we to thank for this place! We'd never have had it but for old Jack. God bless Jack the Ripper, I say!'

Committee, founded in 1882 by well-off Anglo-Jewish women, did home and hospital visiting, and operated much as their Christian peers did. Lady Constance Battersea, a member of the Rothschild family, made weekly trips to Whitechapel and Mile End from her country home for three decades on behalf of another organisation, the Jewish Ladies' Benevolent Loan Society.[7] Toynbee Hall, at the centre of 'Ripper territory', was a nationally known magnet for philanthropic women, despite its official status as a men's settlement. The energetic Henrietta Barnett was central in founding the very successful Children's Country Holiday Fund. The scheme offered children two weeks in the country at modest fees, and an army of volunteers collected small sums weekly all year from each household enrolled. Henrietta's other important programme, the Metropolitan Association for Befriending Young Servants, founded in the 1870s, enlisted more than a thousand well-off women from throughout the metropolis to help find placements as servants for the young girls who left the work-house schools annually, and to follow up on their progress.[8] The Barnetts, as explained below, were also associated with a number of model housing enterprises that were managed by women. Charles Booth's research for his huge study of London life, which began in about 1886 with studies of east London, drew other women in the autumn of 1888: Clara Collet and Beatrice Potter.

The unparalleled numbers of Christian churches and missions (16 of the latter in Whitechapel alone, according to the religious census of London reported in the October 1886 *British Weekly*) enlisted thousands of female volunteers, many from the West End. Indeed Charles Booth, at the turn of the century, claimed that there were at least a hundred 'agencies of a more or less religious and philanthropic character at work in our [east London] district' – more than in any other part of London. He pointed to money raised, church and mission work undertaken on a great scale and 'the self-devotion of very many and the exalted enthusiasm of not a few'. Some agencies used hundreds of volunteers. Just behind Toynbee Hall, in Wentworth

Street, for example, was the non-denominational George Yard Mission for local children, headed by George Holland. To one interviewer Holland claimed that 140 'Christian workers' were involved with the Mission.[9]

The Reverend Thompson's nearby East End Mission, for example, with somewhat fewer volunteers, was one of several urban missions established by the Methodist Conference to reach out to the urban poor as prosperous Methodists exited to the suburbs. The Mission quickly gobbled up a number of old pubs and music halls – including the infamous Paddy's Goose – as well as under-utilised churches, but its centre in Cable Street was about 500 yards from the site of one of the Ripper murders. Thompson, 'shocked and horrified' on learning in 1885 that he was to be the Mission's first head, quickly rallied and within a few years listed over 40 'ladies and gentlemen' who were regular volunteers. Many had been congregation members in Thompson's earlier assigned circuits: twelve came from Blackheath and another 12 from Finsbury Park and Mildmay Park. Every Sunday the Bromhall sisters, one of whom eventually went to China as a missionary, walked over and back from north London. One woman, Miss Salmond, having spent 10 years in Smyrna as a missionary, now worked for the East End Mission six hours a day and established a girls' home and training programme. Another, Alice Seddon, was a Mission volunteer for 43 years, as well as a borough councillor and Poor Law Guardian.[10]

Women's 'slumming' was just part of a cluster of dramatic changes in the lives of women in nineteenth-century Britain. The institution of chaperonage was weakening and women's place in the public realm was gradually expanding – church work and philanthropy being less controversial arenas for women than professions like law or medicine. The development of large urban transportation systems was without a doubt a factor in the story of this phase of female activism. Women had begun to use trains, buses and the Underground to enjoy the shops, museums, restaurants, clubs

and theatres of the city, and these could easily convey a woman from the West End to the East. Kate Potter, second-eldest daughter of a wealthy railway magnate, commuted almost daily from Westminster to Whitechapel in the late 1870s and early 1880s. Later, her younger sister Beatrice went from Chelsea to Tower Bridge by river steamer as well as by train. Women newly at large in the city in the 1880s lacked the confidence of the male spectator – who felt entitled to venture and gawk as he pleased – but neither did the women feel 'the inescapable sense of exposure and trespassing' to be found in women's representations of their urban experiences in earlier decades. Instead, as well-off women reached a critical mass in public spaces and were culturally more acceptable, we find 'the possibility if not the reality of female spectatorship', according to Deborah Nord.[11]

To imagine why young women living in spacious and comfortable homes in town or country would willingly come to the grimmest parts of London requires a look both at the powerful ideals that drew women into districts like Whitechapel, and at what it was in their privileged family circumstances that actually *repelled* so many.

Religious conviction was one of the attracting forces. The Evangelical movement within the established Church as much as in the Nonconformist Churches had long taught a more earnest, personal and practical Christianity. A religious impulse could propel a young woman to volunteer in a mission or church; or to work in secular institutions like settlement houses, hospitals, or dispensaries. Hugh Price Hughes, superintendent of the East End Mission's partner institution in Soho, the West London Mission, was relentless in his efforts to recruit well-off young women to serve God by helping the Soho poor. He and his staff went on speaking tours, and he used

An East End family group, *c*.1900

The Missions were set up to help the East End poor. They provided night shelters, dispensaries, soup kitchens and visited slum dwellers in their homes as well.

193

Whitechapel Road, *c.*1900
The great width of the road was remarked on by visitors as well as the broad pavements.
On a daily basis, thousands of cabs, carts, omnibuses and horse-drawn trams passed to and fro.
Crossing the road was often hazardous.

his high-circulation weekly newspaper to bolster this work. Some West End ministers publicised the settlement movement or other forms of philanthropy and encouraged their parishioners to participate. One of these was the Reverend Hugh Reginald Haweis, who invited Toynbee's Samuel Barnett to talk about the lives and sufferings of his 'poor sinners' in Whitechapel. That is how, in 1876 at the age of 19, overwhelmed by Barnett's powerful rhetoric, Marion Paterson came to call on Mrs Barnett in Whitechapel. Paterson's letter to a friend that year reveals her new fascination.

> I want to go and be their friend: I know they are drunkards and a worse class
> of people than I have ever seen, but I would try so hard to help them if only
> Papa and Mamma will let me . . . The lessons he wants us to teach them are,

'Love one another' and 'Obedience to God'. I feel I must go to them. I know
it will be hard work and most likely seem a failure and their lives will seem so
dreadful to mix with, still I feel I can and ought to do it.[12]

Marion Paterson joined the Barnett household and spent the rest of her life as their
assistant, helper, and informally adopted daughter.

Other women slummers, however, were motivated by an aversion to the routines
of upper-middle-class domestic life. Society rituals establishing 'campaigns of
alliance, inclusion, and social placing', as Leonore Davidoff has put it, placed heavy
burdens on young women living at home. Accompanying their mothers as they
paid calls, answering piles of letters, elaborately dressing and then undressing as
often as five times a day, reading to invalid relatives – these together could generate
excruciating boredom: 'the deadness of the grave' is Lady Aurora's phrase in Henry
James' *Princess Casamassima* (1886).[13] No one stated this grievance more sharply than
Florence Nightingale. 'Living from breakfast till dinner, from dinner till tea, with a
little worsted work, and . . . looking forward to nothing but bed' was her description
of this life, which she poured out in *Cassandra*, her posthumously published plea for
women's freedom to work.[14] Mary Neal, who joined the West London Mission as a
'Sister of the People', in response to Price Hughes' call, was bored by her domestic
round as the daughter of a wealthy Birmingham button manufacturer, but also
offended by the 'pageant of snobbery' of life in a Midlands industrial town, and by
'the complete cleavage between what one really was and liked or disliked, and the
outward life of conventional ideas and conduct'. For example, a family friend, a brass
founder, was listed as a major donor to a missionary society but 'one of his clerks told
us he made a great deal of money by supplying brass idols to be shipped out to
heathen countries'. Within weeks of learning about the formation of the new Sister-
hood, Mary Neal had presented herself. Honnor Morten, nurse, nursing educator and

journalist, was another privileged young woman who rejected the life of a daughter at home. In the 1890s she left her family's sumptuous old Stuart palace at Richmond, though 'all the family forces were mobilized . . . to keep her out of public life'. She established herself in Hoxton, proclaiming her refusal to be 'a fine lady with nothing to do but pay great attention to dress, fashion, and society, and live the humdrum life of the woman who knows and cares nothing about how the other half of the world lives'.[15]

The promise of pleasure also drew women into east London and others of London's poorest districts: the sense of power that comes from gaining a new and specialised knowledge, of usefulness; companionship – with its possibilities of intimacy with others engaged in the same venture, and with working-class subjects themselves; finally, for quite a few, an opportunity to earn their own living. Contemporary novels by the dozen, such as Mary Ward's *Marcella* (1894), portrayed slum work as fascinating and absorbing, a step towards enlightenment. Possibly the best-known slum novel, Walter Besant's *All Sorts and Conditions of Men* (1882), interlaced social reform in east London with the delights of romantic love and the excitement of disguise and mistaken identity. Working in the slums could indeed have an air of romance – in both its 'love' and its 'adventure' meanings – as Beatrice Potter intimated in her diary soon after taking up her duties in 1885 as a rent collector in Smithfield. She referred to 'a certain weird romance, with neither beginning nor end, visiting amongst these people in their dingy homes . . . More often feel envy than pity.' Sister Florence of the East London Mission briskly dissociated herself from the 'romance' of the slums that she recognised women like her expected to enjoy. Speaking to a large public meeting in 1891, she denied that a search for adventure or novelty or 'romantic conceptions of life' had drawn her to east London. Indeed, she was surrounded by heart-breaking sin and misery – not romance – yet was one of the 'happiest people on earth'.[16]

This photograph by John Galt of around 1900 shows the work of the all-male London City Mission going about its work in the East End calling door-to-door and helping the poor. Tom Pearson, a 'missionary', is accompanied by two women helpers.

Many women considered their slum years a turning-point, deepening their understanding and helping them to mature. As Mary Neal, later a folk music and music education expert, wrote of her time (1888–95) as a Sister at the West London Mission: those years 'have left an indelible mark on my mind and spirit, and coloured the attitude which I cannot help taking on social and economic problems'. She contrasts with pride her 'actual experience face to face with those suffering under economic conditions' with the ideas about social questions 'inspired by academic

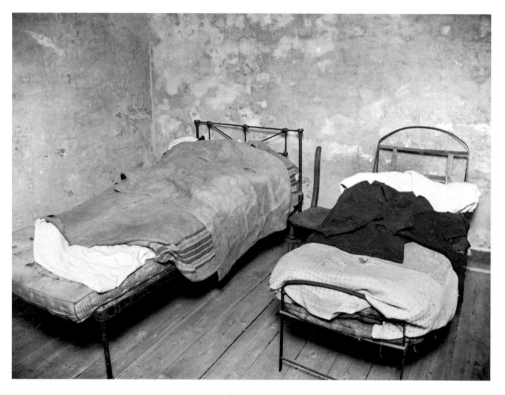

Room with two beds, *c.*1905

Reminiscent of the photography of Walker Evans, the two beds in an empty room can be viewed as symbolising the terrible living conditions of London's poor. The bare walls and the two old rickety iron-framed beds with dirty mattresses and blankets seem to be waiting the arrival of their nightly exhausted visitors. A single broken chair divides the two beds.

knowledge learned from books and lectures'.[17] Her co-worker as a Sister and lifelong friend Emmeline Pethick-Lawrence, best known as a suffragist, similarly wrote of the emancipation of mental and practical powers which is to be found by working as 'a free person in a community of equals'. On Pethick's very first morning at the Mission she knew that 'a new life of the spirit' was beginning.[18]

Freedom from the restrictions and artificiality of their home lives provided the liveliest of satisfactions. Honnor Morten, the Richmond escapee, 'merriest of saints', exulted in her independence. In her room in Hoxton she was 'right in the centre of life'. She took great pleasure in being seen as 'friends and neighbours' by the surrounding households. Her interviewer for a Christian magazine for girls, *Young Woman*, put special emphasis on housework. She did 'scrubbing, washing, cooking, marketing, and all the rest . . .' Morten insisted: 'You must level your expenditure down to theirs, and then see how you like it.' Morten's own position was unequivo-cal: 'Yes, I like it.' She expected 'Romance' at any moment, she jokes, and 'Romance walked up first in the shape of the curate', who was unsuspectingly paying a visit with soup-tickets. Morten's semi-fictional character Drusilla taunts him by telling him that she didn't go to church, and then gave him a scholarly critique, using Greek, of the concept of the incarnation. 'The curate left suddenly,' she says triumphantly.[19]

Beatrice Potter, fully aware of but deeply conflicted about her own attraction for the gowns, balls, and dinners of the London Season, was fleeing that life and yearning for a more productive one. Potter did not have the ebullience of Honnor Morten, nor her gleeful amusement at such new experiences as sweeping out her own flat. Yet she conveys her delight in her description of an excursion to Victoria Park and vicinity in 1887 with friends Ella Pycroft and Kerrigan, an Irish-born School Board visitor. Afterwards, Kerrigan entertained them in his room. His was a single

A Salvation Army shelter for women in [Hanbury Street] Whitechapel, drawn from life by Paul Renouard, the Graphic, *27 February 1892.*
'In the dormitory itself, over the supports of the upper dormitory or gallery, is the awful question, in red and white, "Are you ready to die?" When the night is still, half the inmates surely look as though they were dead already; the unsightly receptacles for the sleepers are strangely like open coffins – open graves – in which repose and rest in peace for awhile – some of them – these weary, hard-driven offshoots of our poor humanity.'

room, 'the back room of a small working-class dwelling – serving . . . with the most ingenious arrangements for all his functions'. She wrote in her journal:

> Ah! What would the conventional West End acquaintance say to two young women smoking and talking in the bed, sitting, working, smoking and bath room of an East End School Board visitor? It is quite sad leaving the homely 'Quaker' hotel [on Bishopsgate, where she often stayed]. Ella Pycroft and I have found each other excellent company. We have entertained freely and thoroughly enjoyed our life in working-class society.[20]

The lady's arrival in her slum was not always so delightful, of course – though women's negative experiences were usually kept out of agency newsletters and annual reports. Seth Koven's emphasis on 'dirt', a subject of both horror and fascination, as 'a pervasive trope in women's writings about the slums and themselves', is well taken. Beatrice Webb certainly made no secret in her autobiography – published in 1926 – of her dislike of the slovenly and disorderly lives she encountered among the Whitechapel poor, and soured quickly on the idea of a career among them. Said Mary Neal, also in an autobiography written years later, of her first months as a Sister, 'My idea of hell has always been a place of noise and cold, and this first winter in London certainly fulfilled these conditions and nothing but a sort of dogged desire not to give in enabled me to go through with the work which I was given to do.' One of the first religious services she attended in Soho filled her with 'despair': it was packed with 'dirty and miserable' men. And 'leg slapping' was the hymns' only accompaniment. Often Sister Mary was close to 'being sick with the stench and horror of the condition of those I had seen in the room'. Alice Hodson, at Lady Margaret Hall settlement in south London a little later, wrote of her distress at the insistent noise of trams, buses and market carts; the dirt – dust, fog and smuts which reached 'the innermost recesses of your being'; and the smells of 'much-worn

Poor East End children, *c.*1900

The eldest daughter was often left to look after the family when her parents were out at work.
Such 'little mothers' were regular parts of east London neighbourhoods.

clothes, very questionable cooking, and human beings crowded into a small space', as well as the filthy bedding and messy uncleared tables.[21]

Yet hundreds, more likely thousands, of well-off women were at home in the 'Ripper's London'. Female housing managers — often derisively termed 'lady rent collectors' — were ubiquitous figures in east London with its high complement of model dwellings. The idea that well-bred women would make good managers of slum buildings had originated with Octavia Hill as early as the 1860s when she

 A knife-grinder and a cat's meat man, c.1905

The cat's meat man with his basket sold cheap meat as pet food because there were so few household leftovers to feed the pets. Often horsemeat, it was unfit for human consumption and sometimes even too rotten for pets. The knife-grinders with their barrows were a common sight on the streets of the East End. One of their ruses was to sharpen scissors for a fixed sum and, having unscrewed them, decline to put them together again without further payment.

Homeless men near the Embankment and entering a midnight soup kitchen, *c.*1902
Homeless men, many from the East End, turned up at Missions and refuges in the West End
looking for food and night shelter. The location of this soup kitchen was opposite the
St Giles Christian Mission that occupied the disused and shortly to be demolished
Olympic Theatre in Wych Street, Strand.

undertook to remodel and administer a group of very run-down cottages in
Marylebone. Her operations expanded to other districts, though she eventually let
others take charge of the new buildings near Toynbee Hall. The managers spent
about two days a week at each of their buildings. Eight women helped to manage the
property that the Barnetts and their associates had bought or built in this zone by the

1880s: New Court; the George Yard Buildings (where a murdered woman was found in mid-August); Brunswick Buildings in Goulston Street (completed in 1886), and the Wentworth Buildings (also 1886) in Wentworth Street; along with the Katherine Buildings further south in East Smithfield near Tower Bridge, which the East End Dwellings Company opened in 1885; and, in 1887, the Company's College Buildings on the site of Crown Court.[22]

Housing managers moved right through the Ripper's turf as they went from building to building collecting rents, querying references for prospective tenants or taking money to the bank. Margaret Nevinson, one of them, later a writer, suffragist and magistrate, describes an uncomfortable stop in the late 1880s at a 'thieves'

Street traders in Whitechapel Road, *c.* 1910
All these men had been trained as street hawkers by the Whitechapel Mission.
The man on the left was an old soldier.

kitchen' in Flower and Dean Street while carrying a large bag of rent cash. Kate Potter, the second-eldest of the nine Potter sisters, managed two buildings from 1876 until 1883. Miss Busk, another early east-London manager, might have given the Ripper a run for his money; she was six feet tall and 'as brave and buoyant as she was big'. Early in 1885 Kate's younger sister Beatrice began her duties as a manager in the Wentworth Dwellings and in the newly erected Katherine Buildings (named in Kate's honour). She thus joined a group of east-London-based 'glorified spinsters', as a journalist had termed them, women who had chosen working lives over marriage. Potter's early months in east London looking into prospective tenants' references involved 'long trudges through Whitechapel leaving her "utterly *done*"'. Potter remained in this post for just a few years, while Ella Pycroft, her fellow Smithfield rent collector, remained until 1890. Also there is Clementina Black's sister Constance, who, though not a housing manager but a librarian at the People's Palace, had taken two rooms in the College Buildings in 1887. When she married Edward Garnett, the two continued to live there.[23]

By the autumn of 1888, Potter had been traversing east London for nearly four years, first as a housing manager and then as a Charles Booth researcher. Working on a study of the London Docks in 1887, she met School Board visitors for Millwall and Limehouse, managers and employees at some of the docks and riverside wharves (St Katharine's Dock, and West India Dock, Millwall Dock and Fresh Wharf). She watched the early morning scramble of casual labourers for a day's work, went to the Peabody Dwellings where many dock labourers lived, visited a wool warehouse, and spent sociable evenings in the St George's Yard club for London and St Katharine's Docks' 'preferable' men. For a study of the garment industry, in autumn of 1887, using connections through a family of Jewish Katherine Buildings tenants, Potter began to learn 'how to sweat' with the help of the Moses family of Oxford Street, Stepney. In the spring of 1888 she took lodgings at 56 Great Prescott Street and, disguised as a young working woman, began hunting for employment in Princes Street and Wood Street tailors' shops. She had to travel further east, to 198 Mile End Road, where she was finally hired, and worked for a few days in a Jewish-owned shop. She published her account of this experience as 'Pages from a Work-girl's Diary' in the *Nineteenth Century* (September 1888).[24]

Potter was out of town at the height of the Ripper fear, returning on 31 October. In November and December 1888, she was hard at work on her study of east

Annie Besant, 1891
Photograph by Herbert Barraud,
published by Eglington & Co.

London's Jewish community, 'seeing Jews of all classes all day long', using the Devonshire Hotel on Bishopsgate as her headquarters. She journeyed to Petticoat Lane, went to the Jewish Working Men's Club, and met several other Booth researchers at Toynbee Hall, including Clara Collet, who was beginning her own research for Booth.[25] Potter did not mention the murder in her extensive diaries, but the sympathetic tone of her study on London's Jewish community might be her own response to the anti-Jewish rumours and vigilantism of the early weeks of the Ripper episode. Potter's study is relatively free of anti-Semitic stereotyping, and dismissive of the standard positions on the harm of Jewish 'sweaters' to the English economy.

Annie Besant, having helped the match workers in Mile End, initially 1,500 of them, with their successful strike in the summer, was another lady very much in evidence in east London during the Ripper months. Her mission was to defeat her Conservative opponent, Claude Montefiore, for a position on the London School Board for the Tower Hamlets division. The election took place towards the end of November so Besant was especially busy in October and November. Her platform included free school dinners, no school fees, secular education, and School Board contracts at union rates of pay. Besant's campaign was vigorous and flamboyant. She drove around the district in a dogcart with a red ribbon in her hair, relishing the fierce opposition she elicited from local Anglican clergymen, vestrymen and other members of the east London male establishment. George Bernard Shaw described her election meetings as 'unique and luminous in the

Repairing garments, Whitechapel Mission's Brunswick Hall night shelter, *c.*1910
One of the aims of the Mission was to provide more than temporary relief for the poor and
unemployed. It was found that many failed to find work because of their ragged appearance.
Old jackets and trousers were mended and cleaned.

squalid record of London electioneering'.[26] Her Anglo-Jewish opponent had Jewish
supporters, but socialist-leaning Jewish workers supported Besant. Labour leader
Lewis Lyons (whom she had once bailed out of jail) was highly effective in rallying
Yiddish-speaking voters to her side. Besant also had the support of the local MP,
Samuel Montagu. An enthusiastic rally on her behalf took place the day before the
last murder, on 8 November 1888, at the Stepney Meeting Hall, off Stepney Green.
Besant won the election handily, coming top of the poll with over 15,000 votes.[27] In the
same month she had a second victory: the resignation of Police Commissioner Sir
Charles Warren, against whom she had waged a vigorous campaign because of his

military-overkill handling of the Trafalgar Square 'Bloody Sunday' demonstration of 13 November 1887.

'Dinner hour with factory girls' was an established form of philanthropy mentioned in manuals for would-be charity-givers, and the hope of doing this in Whitechapel attracted Margo Tennant, a wealthy Anglo-Scottish socialite, whose other passions were golf and horses. In 1894 she would marry the Home Secretary Herbert Asquith. She was journeying regularly to Whitechapel in the autumn of 1888. The recent death of her beloved religious and philanthropic sister Laura, with whom she had been presented into society in 1881,[28] drove her to the East End where she spent much of her time walking around. She was eventually attracted to a cardboard box factory with a heavily young and female workforce. Imperiously, she asked to be shown in to the proprietor, Clifford, and explained that allowing her to enter to speak to his employees would be a favour to her as she was 'so very unhappy' herself. Tennant visited the factory regularly until her marriage, her thrice-weekly visits interspersed with West End shopping and with months at the family estate in Scotland. With some of the factory girls she visited the nearby scene of one of the Whitechapel murders, blandly commenting years later: 'It was strange watching crowds of people collected daily to see nothing but an archway.'[29]

A more purposeful visitor to Whitechapel was Clementina Black, activist on behalf of working women. Black, an officer in the newly named Women's Trades Union Provident League, had been, along with Besant, assisting the Bryant and May match workers. On 8 July Black was among the speakers at a strikers' mass meeting on the Mile End Waste, and later in the month she was on the committee drawing up the by-laws for the new union, which the union representatives viewed and discussed at the Stepney Meeting Hall. Meanwhile, she wrote and spoke on behalf of the match workers all over London. In early September Clementina Black was out of town, at the annual meeting of the Trades Union Congress, and was involved in the strike efforts of a group of Leeds women. On 2 November, though, she was back in London, and, along with other labour leaders, spoke to a 'large contingent' of young women cigar-makers at St Jude's School, adjacent to Toynbee Hall. There she urged them to form their union at once to prevent their wages going down.[30]

Margaret Harkness was a cousin of Beatrice Potter and one of her 'glorified spinsters' – though, unlike Potter, Harkness had been cut off by her father and needed to earn her own living. Harkness too was in Whitechapel in 1888, but spent some time in Scotland as well. She lived off and on at the Katherine Buildings, showing the neighbourhood to her friend Eleanor Marx and gathering materials for articles she was writing and editing for the *British Weekly*, a Christian periodical. She is one of the few women visitors to have commented directly on the Ripper case. Under her pseudonym John Law, she wrote a letter to the *Pall Mall Gazette* deploring the Whitechapel Road Wax Museum's 'ghastly display of the unfortunate woman murdered by what the slummers [her word for slum-dwellers] call "that bloody demon" . . .' After the Ripper murders began, Harkness writes, the museum's managers immediately modified some of their existing human figures, covering them liberally with gashes and gory red paint. Children were among the most enthusiastic viewers, which was obviously unsuitable, as 'a smell of death rises into your nostrils, and you feel as if your throat were filled up by fungus'. Harkness knew the museum well, depicting one like it, the 'East London Palace of Royal Waxworks', in the novel, *Captain Lobe*, she was writing that year. Her fictional waxworks was worse than its real counterparts. It housed, among its other attractions, a display of murderers and victims that elicited screams from the spectators and made the heroine gasp for air. *Captain Lobe*, a story about Salvationists and socialists set mainly in Whitechapel, was being published in instalments by the *British Weekly* between late April and the end of December 1888, so the novel's grizzly wax museum surely exemplified the display she found so repugnant in reality.[31]

An East End fairground, *c*.1900
Freak shows and waxworks were found along Whitechapel Road. In September 1888,
just days after one of the Jack the Ripper murders, there was a waxwork with depictions of
the mutilated and murdered victim.

A recent biography of Clara Collet includes a chapter titled 'Jack the Ripper and Charles Booth', though Collet had direct contact only with the latter. Collet was Charles Booth's final choice to write a section on women's work for his 'London Life and Labour' project, and her education and interests – and need for a job – made her the perfect candidate. So Clara moved to east London in November 1888 (her address there is not known) and began learning about the trades that employed women in factories and workshops, and as home workers. As one of her research methods, according to Booth, Collet disguised herself as a working-class woman, met girls at their workplaces, befriended them, and then invited them to her own house. She also interviewed ladies from missions and philanthropic clubs and other programmes for girls. Thus for three months Collet was combing the area, sometimes accompanied by Booth's assistant George Arkell, and sometimes alone. Her article on women's work in Booth's book shows what some of her destinations were. She wrote about tailoring and children's suits in Whitechapel and cotton sunshade makers 'in the neighbourhood of Petticoat Lane'. Her finished report, first published in the 1889 edition, has nothing to say about the violence in the area but a little more about prostitution, which she saw mainly in relation to women's low wages. She discusses what we would now call sexual harassment by foremen. She refers to the 'immorality of many of these younger fur-sewers' as a function of their trade's irregularity and mentions lower-middle-class girls' greater temptation to 'sin for the externals which they have learnt to regard as essentials'.[32]

Eleanor Marx, daughter of Karl, born into the international socialist movement, can also be classed as a London 'lady', a friend of many of the Whitechapel wanderers already mentioned: Clara Collet, Annie Besant, Margaret Harkness, Clementina Black and the poet Amy Levy. She had come to east London as what her first biographer calls 'an explorer', and to Whitechapel at some point in 1888 with Margaret Harkness. These experiences engendered in Eleanor for the first time an

Eleanor Marx, 1881
*Pencil drawing by Grace Black
(later Grace Human).*

intense connection with English workers. She was in the United States with Edward Aveling until the end of September 1888, and was then busy organising the Second International meeting in Paris. But in 1889 she began her journeys to east London in earnest, first in Canning Town (in summer and autumn 1889) assisting Will Thorne and the striking Becton gas workers – she had become 'quite an East Ender' by then. She added to this the dock strike in the summer of 1889, when Marx and Margaret Harkness, the only two women to do so, daily travelled out to assist the strike committee. Eleanor was also involved with striking workers at Silver's India Rubber Works just east of the Tower Hamlets border. She commuted daily to Silvertown, 'that out-of-the-world place', throughout the autumn until the strike ended, unsuccessfully, in mid-December 1889. In 1890 she was closer to Whitechapel, speaking on Mile End Waste, in a protest meeting against a new wave of persecutions of Jews in Russia – possibly her first official statement as a Jew. For the rest of her sadly truncated life (she died, a suicide, in 1898) Eleanor Marx was an active trade union organiser throughout London, and so involved with Whitechapel's Jewish garment workers that she had taught herself how to give public speeches in Yiddish.[33]

Thus, along with women with agendas to rescue or convert prostitutes, a variety of accomplished and dedicated women shared the Ripper's turf without fear or concern as they carried out their own tasks. The east London of the 1880s, despite

South side of Christ Church, Spitalfields, *c.*1900
The iron fence of 'Itchy Park' can be seen on the right. Just two streets to the south lay
Flower and Dean Street and directly to the west was Dorset Street. This area was at the
centre of what has been called the East End's 'dark ghetto'.

its worldwide notoriety, cannot simply be described as a region of poverty, danger and degradation. A showcase of creative philanthropy and evangelical religion, home of a remarkable and growing Jewish community, and a bustling industrial centre, Whitechapel was also a magnet for earnest, energetic and restless women – and men. The efforts of so many to improve conditions in east London were only sometimes successful and certainly not always welcomed by their proposed beneficiaries. Yet they represent a significant aspect of the Ripper story, and an important episode in the history of women in Britain as the modern era was finally dawning for them.

217

CHAPTER SIX

MAPPING THE EAST END LABYRINTH

LAURA VAUGHAN

INTRODUCTION: THE IMAGINED GHETTO

The Old Nichol district was one of the worst slums in the East End area. Following its demolition, the surviving streets and alleys were described by the social reformer Henrietta Barnett:

> None of these courts had roads. In some the houses were three storeys high and hardly six feet apart, the sanitary accommodation being pits in the cellars; in other courts the houses were lower, wooden and dilapidated, a stand pipe at the end providing the only water. Each chamber was the home of a family who sometimes owned their indescribable furniture . . . In many instances broken windows had been repaired with paper and rags, the banisters had been used for firewood, and the paper hung from the walls which were the residence of countless vermin.[1]

This account of the state of decay and deprivation present in the East End in 1888 provides a sober contrast to the typically lurid images provided in the popular press at

1 An East End Street. *Photograph by John Galt, c.1900*

the time. The east London of Jack the Ripper is similarly portrayed today, with colourful descriptions of the sinister dark alleys of the city of that time. But are these perceptions correct? Might an approach that systematically describes and analyses the streets of London's East End shed some light on the nature of the 'dark ghetto'?

East London in 1888 was an overcrowded, densely packed district, suffering from some of the highest rates of poverty in the city. One of the most important sources for the situation on the ground at the time, Charles Booth's *Descriptive Map of London Poverty 1889*, was published as part of his famous series of books: *Life and Labour of the People in London*. This map covered the extent of built-up London and presented the social conditions of the people of London according to seven classes. Booth, an industrialist and social philanthropist, had set out to conduct a scientific inquiry into the economic and industrial situation on a street-by-street basis. There were in fact three published maps.

The first, published in 1889 and showing the poverty situation of the East End only, was the result of a house-to-house survey conducted by Charles Booth and his team in 1886.

The second map, the first to cover an extensive area of London, the *Descriptive Map of London Poverty 1889*, was a map of social conditions more than poverty. It represented a combination of factors such as regularity of income, work status and industrial occupation (because some occupations were seasonal and thus irregular). This map was coloured according to finely delineated gradations of poverty and prosperity, differentiating between street blocks – and on occasion street sides – and was based on data collected by Booth and his team of researchers, which included School Board Visitors, who had a detailed knowledge of families with children. The Visitors' information was cross-checked against reports by philanthropists, social workers, policemen and others, which along with Booth's own assessments provided as scientific a record as was available at the time.[2]

For the third map, *Descriptive Map of London Poverty 1898–9*, members of the Booth Inquiry went on 'walks' around the area – usually with a policeman – recording in vivid language their impressions of how the streets had changed since 1889.

The importance of the Booth maps is their graphic power in showing to the public and to the politicians of the time the true nature and extent of poverty in London. Booth used his scientific approach of quantifying poverty and visualising its spread to make specific recommendations for urban reforms. He stressed the importance of providing more open space for recreation, and the benefit of opening up the hemmed-in poverty areas. He also used his influence to suggest the introduction of old-age pensions, and revisions to the census to allow data to be gathered on overcrowding which he viewed as vital to obtaining more accurate figures on population numbers in poor areas as well as for measuring poverty itself.

Even the briefest of looks at Booth's maps, the first of which coincides almost perfectly with the year of the Ripper murders, shows a distribution of prosperity to poverty in a pattern that closely follows a sequence: squares and avenues were more prosperous than thoroughfares, roads and streets, which were more prosperous than alleys, courts and yards, which were not as poverty stricken as dead ends and rookeries. In other words, the smaller and more confined and hedged-in the area, the poorer it was.

It was not only fine-scale layout which had an impact on social conditions, creating pockets of irregularity in the urban grid. Larger-scale obstacles in the urban fabric had a deleterious effect on the ability of people to move around and improve their social and economic conditions. Booth frequently noted in his writing that physical boundaries such as railways had the effect of isolating areas, walling off their inhabitants and cutting them off from the life of the city. The urban historian H. J. Dyos has pointed out 'how often these introspective places were seized by the "criminal classes", whose professional requirements were isolation, an entrance that could be watched and a back exit kept exclusively for the getaway . . .' Dyos describes how

Booth's maps show how minor changes to the street layout often reinforced the tendency of poor areas to be severed from the outside world. Such changes 'acted like tourniquets applied too long, and below them gangrene almost invariably set in . . . it was sometimes possible to run through the complete declension from meadow to slum in a single generation, or even less'.[3] Gareth Stedman Jones has also noted that

> One great effect of railway, canals and docks in cutting into human communities [is] a psychological one . . . East Londoners showed a tendency to become decivilised when their back streets were cut off from main roads by railway embankments . . . Savage communities in which drunken men and women fought daily in the streets were far harder to clear up, if walls or water surrounded the area on three sides, leaving only one entrance.[4]

Booth, Dyos and Stedman Jones all point towards the possibility that changes to the urban layout can itself contribute to areas of poverty sinking into even greater decline. Scientific research into this subject has been taking place for the past thirty years within the field of 'space syntax', which uses architectural research methods as tools for studying built space and society.

THE STREETSCAPE OF POVERTY

The study of the physical form of the city and its relationship to poverty helps us understand the East End in 1888. Research into Booth's map of 1889 has found a strong relationship between the spatial location of poverty and a relative lack of physical accessibility. Yet the separation between poor and more prosperous streets was not as sharp as previously thought. Although there were pockets of severe deprivation, these were frequently located in close proximity to more affluent areas.[5]

222

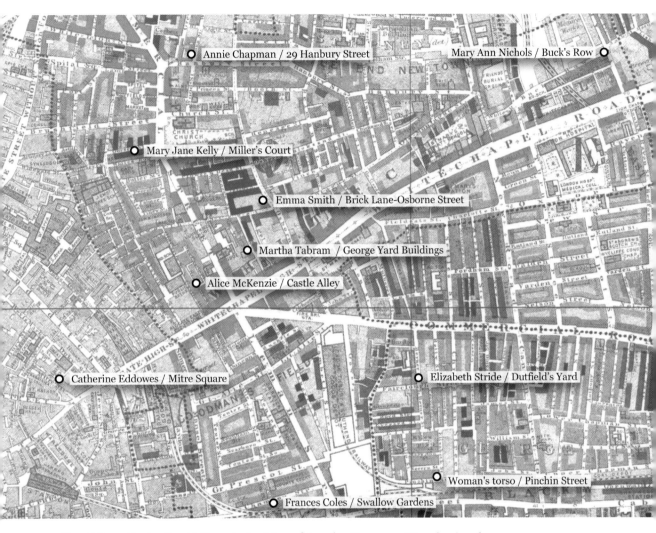

Annie Chapman / 29 Hanbury Street

Mary Ann Nichols / Buck's Row

Mary Jane Kelly / Miller's Court

Emma Smith / Brick Lane-Osborne Street

Martha Tabram / George Yard Buildings

Alice McKenzie / Castle Alley

Catherine Eddowes / Mitre Square

Elizabeth Stride / Dutfield's Yard

Woman's torso / Pinchin Street

Frances Coles / Swallow Gardens

Detail from Charles Booth's Descriptive Map of London Poverty, 1889, *showing the location of the Whitechapel murders*

- ■ Lowest class, Vicious, Semi-criminal.
- ■ Very poor, Casual, Chronic want.
- □ Poor. 18s. to 21s. a week for a moderate family.
- ■ Mixed. Some comfortable, others poor.
- ■ Fairly comfortable. Good ordinary earnings.
- ■ Middle class. Well to do.
- □ Upper middle and Upper classes. Wealthy.

SPACE SYNTAX

Space syntax is a theory of space and a set of analytical, quantitative and descriptive tools for analysing the layout of space in buildings and cities. Originating in the Bartlett School of Architecture, University College London in the 1970s, it started with an attempt to understand if there was an underlying architectural explanation for the social failure of twentieth-century English housing estates. The research field aims to answer key architectural and urban design questions, starting with whether the layout of cities has an impact on how people use streets.

Space syntax analysis is concerned with systematically describing and analysing streets, squares and all open public space as a continuous system in order to measure how well connected each street space is to its surroundings. This is done by taking an accurate map and drawing a set of intersecting lines through all the spaces of the urban grid so that the grid is covered and all rings of circulation are completed. The resulting set of lines is called an 'axial map'.

Space syntax analysis computes all the lines according to their relative depth to each other, using simple mathematical measures. The terminology used to describe this depth states how spatially *integrated* or *segregated* it is. The resulting numbers then form the basis for coloured-up maps which represent the distribution of spatial accessibility. The range of numbers goes from red for the most accessible (integrated) through the colour spectrum to blue for the least accessible (segregated) (PLATE 9).

By examining space in this way it is possible to analyse the correspondence between spatial segregation/integration and social statistics. For example, the relationship between the location of burglaries and housing layout can be researched; or, whether more successful shopping streets have spatial characteristics in common. This is done by using statistical analysis to measure the correspondence between spatial and social measures.

High

Low

PLATE 9. *Space syntax maps of the East End showing distribution of integration in 1889. Detail of the vicinity of Dorset Street* (top) *and Whitechapel and Spitalfields area* (bottom) *with murder locations marked by red circles.*

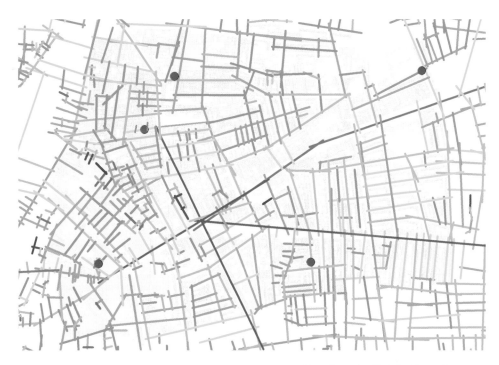

Maps drawn by Christian Beros-Contreros.

Lowest class, Vicious, Semi-criminal.

Very poor, Casual, Chronic want.

Poor. 18s. to 21s. a week for a moderate family.

Mixed. Some comfortable, others poor.

Fairly comfortable. Good ordinary earnings.

Middle class. Well to do.

Upper middle and Upper classes. Wealthy.

PLATE 10. *Detail from Booth's* Map of Poverty *(1889) showing the Dorset Street area* (top) *and Whitechapel and Spitalfields area* (bottom) *with murder locations marked by red circles.*

Nonconformist Church ✖
Fully Licensed House ◉
Beer House 'on'-'off' license ◎
Beer House 'off' license ○
Grocers with alcohol license ✚
Board School ▪
Nonconformist & Unsectarian Church ✕
Church of England Mission ✚
Jewish Synagogue S
Church of England +
Voluntary School ▲
Roman Catholic Church ✳
Restaurant with alcohol license ◉

PLATE 11. *Map showing religious worship sites, public elementary schools and licensed houses, c.1899–1900. Dorset Street area* (top) *and Whitechapel and Spitalfields area* (bottom) *with murder locations marked by red circles.*

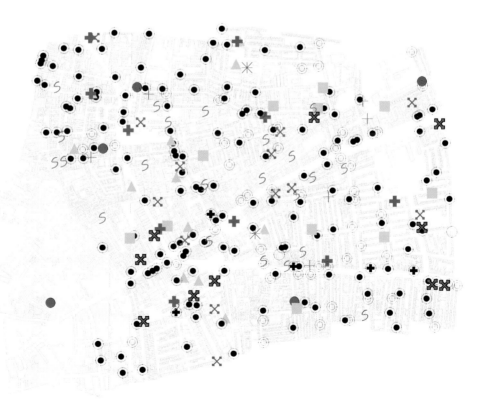

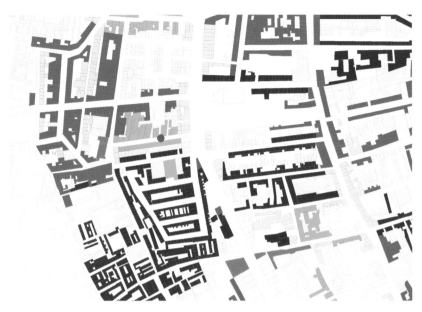

95% to 100%
75% and less than 95%
50% and less than 75%
25% and less than 50%
5% and less than 25%
less than 5%

PLATE 12. *Map showing Jewish population proportions, adapted from the map published in* The Jew in London, *Russell and Lewis (1900). Dorset Street area* (top) *and Whitechapel and Spitalfields area* (bottom) *with murder locations marked by red circles.*

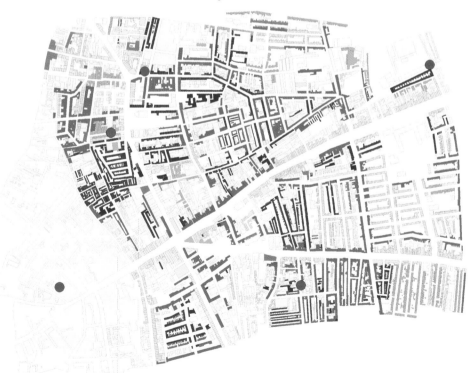

PLATE 13. *Dorset Street area,*
Goad Fire Insurance plan,
Vol.11, sheet 34, May 1890.

SCALE 40'=1"

PLATE 14. *Detail from the* Modern Plague of London *map, published in the mid 1880s by the National Temperance movement. Many Victorians saw alcohol as the major cause of ill health, poverty and moral degradation. Public houses and the temperance movement competed for the loyalty of London's working classes. There were 48 pubs in a one-mile section of the Whitechapel Road.*

PLATE 15. *Spitalfields and Whitechapel, detail from Charles Booth's original hand-coloured* Map of Poverty, *c.1888–9. The City of London, with its relatively small day-time population, was not covered by the survey.*

The situation in the East End was more complex still if we consider the mix of people living there at the time. In the 1880s the area contained two principal minority groups: Irish and Jewish.

J. A. Jackson has described how the Irish influx had started a generation earlier with the famine of the 1840s, when many Irish migrants arrived in British ports 'destitute, starving and often diseased'.[6] By 1851 the number of Irish-born in London had risen to almost 110,000. Due to a range of difficulties to do with their lack of skills and their abject poverty, coupled with prejudice, the Irish immigrants were still suffering from deprivation at the time of the Ripper murders. Another authority, Lynn Lees, has shown that many of the immigrants failed to move on from the East End because the poorest families had to remain close to where work was available.[7]

The other significant group in the area was that of the Jewish immigrants, who, like the mainly Catholic Irish, had achieved emancipation only relatively recently. Although Jewish resettlement in England is normally dated from 1656, settlement in London in general and the East End of London in particular was limited until 1881. Jewish settlement in Britain, especially in major port cities, gained momentum in the early 1880s. Some Jews were driven by economic hardship from the Pale of Settlement (an area on the western edge of the Russian Empire established in 1771 to prevent the Jews of White Russia from spreading throughout Russia), others were victims of anti-Semitic pogroms. Thus waves of Jewish refugees arrived from Eastern Europe, intensifying the existing established settlement in London from 1882 onwards. Although the Jewish immigrants, when they arrived, were as poor as the Irish incomers, some of them had an advantage as coming from a more urbanised and craft-skilled population. They quickly filled a narrow range of home-based workshop occupations, such as tailoring and boot- and shoe-making, which enabled small-scale employment within the immigrant community. Still, there is clear evidence of the extent of Jewish poverty: for example in an article from the *Spectator* in 1887,[8] figures are given stating that every third Jew in London was in receipt of poor relief and every second Jew belonged to the regular pauper class. Much of this neediness was due to the seasonal nature of their occupations, which meant a precarious existence.

Whitechapel was one of the poorest districts in London, with one of the largest concentrations of lodging-houses. Yet it is also important to note that the district had a wide variety of poverty, as is evident from the Booth maps. The influx of Jewish immigrants in the 1880s provided new unskilled jobs and this influx, coupled with the street layout that contained a fine grain of poverty and relative prosperity cheek by jowl, created high economic interdependence between relatively well-off and very poor.[9] Despite perceptions of the immigrants as living a 'ghettoised' life separate from the existing population, spatial analysis coupled with historical evidence suggests that the situation was much more complex: there is likely to have been considerable contact between the two populations.[10][11]

'THE WORST STREET I HAVE SEEN SO FAR'

A striking illustration of the ability of maps to shed light on the spatial context of the area can be found in the Goad Fire Insurance plans. From the 1880s the Goad Company was dominant in the field of fire insurance plans and they used large-scale (1 in. = 40 ft) plans to record their surveys of risk across Britain, concentrating on major towns and cities. They used a wide range of colours, signs and symbols to show information such as building materials (brick, stone or concrete; wood, metal or timber), windows, building heights, roofs and skylights as well as street widths and the precise building footprint. In addition, building use (shop, dwelling and so on) was recorded. The surveys were undertaken on a five-yearly basis (and in some cases more frequently) to capture information on the level of fire risk – such as a hay store

Dorset Street, *c*.1902, taken from Jack London's *People of the Abyss*

as opposed to a boot factory – as well as to record the spatial concentration of policy holders of individual insurance companies.

One of the murder victims attributed to Jack the Ripper, Mary Jane Kelly, is believed to have been aged around 25 and, like the other victims, in poverty at the time of her death in November 1888. Bill Fishman records that the murdered body of Mary Jane Kelly was found in a 'filthy one-roomed dwelling at No. 9 of the enclosed Miller's Court off Dorset Street'. The Goad Fire Insurance map for the Dorset Street area (PLATE 13) shows that Miller's Court was an extremely narrow, enclosed courtyard surrounded by two-storey brick-built dwellings. It was entered from a roof-tiled passageway leading north from Dorset Street. The street, coloured on the Booth map

227

as black, 'vicious, semi-criminal', can be seen on the Goad plan as comprising run-down low-rent tenement houses, extensive lodging-houses to accommodate the itin-erant poor and only a handful of shops and public houses. Dorset Street's western end faced the Providence Row Night Refuge and School, and to the east it faced the wider, better-lit expanses of Commercial Street. The Goad plan suggests that the route from Commercial Street would not have been well observed late at night, with a boot factory and public house framing the entrance from the main road, leading past shops on Dorset Street, with only the dwellings overlooking Miller's Court itself likely to have provided any witnesses. On a larger scale, the plan illustrates the wide range of housing and building types in the area, from shops and small warehouses and factories with dwellings over on Commercial Street to lodging-houses in Dorset Street and White's Row.

Miller's Court was just two turnings away from Commercial Street, which contained workshops and tailoring establishments employing the skilled and semi-skilled inhabitants of the area. Overlaid on the map of building layout at the time (redrawn from the Booth maps) is an extract from a 'space syntax' map of spatial accessibility coloured in shades from red to dark blue to represent values on a scale ranging from integrated to segregated. It is notable, on the one hand, that Dorset Street is coloured in the middle to high tones of the scale, indicating relatively high levels of accessibility and indeed the street itself was only a few steps off Commercial Street, one of the main streets in the district. But the court itself was more segregated, with a lower level of accessibility. This is typical of the street layout of the time, with a juxtaposition of segregated back alleys a few turnings away from the local main street. Looking at the map, it is evident how the spatial structure of the area created the possibility for busy and quiet streets to be located in close proximity.[12] The location of the murder site quite close to Commercial Street is not surprising, bearing in mind that the perpetrator probably met his victims on relatively busy streets. On the other hand, in order to carry out the murder, he needed the relative quiet of the back alleys of the area – in this case, Mary Jane Kelly's single-room lodging in Miller's Court. When we look at the location of the other murder sites, a similar spatial structure is revealed, with the streets typically being in the medium to low colour range, but not completely segregated, as might have been envisaged.

Taking into consideration the social and economic situation of the surrounding streets, we see in the illustration showing the murder location in relation to Booth's classification of poverty classes that there was a dramatic drop in economic situation between the dwellings and shops on Commercial Street – coloured red – and the buildings in the alleys and courts just a few steps away, which were coloured in the lowest classification of black[13] (PLATE 10).

As mentioned earlier, Booth's social investigators revisited the categorisation of the streets for the revised maps published in 1899. By accompanying the local police on their beats around the streets of London, they were able to update the maps from the policemen's local knowledge as well as their own observations. The notebooks of the walks provide vivid detail on the physical situation, housing types and conditions as well as the degree of poverty of the people living in the streets, and whether these had changed since publication of the 1889 edition. Dorset Street was revisited in 1898 and Booth's investigator writes in his notebook that it had been classified black in 1888, and was still classified as black in 1898:

> The worst street I have seen so far. Thieves, prostitutes, bullies. All common lodging houses. Some called 'doubles' with double beds for married couples, but merely another name for brothels: women, draggled, torn skirts, dirty, unkempt . . . Jews standing about in street or on doorsteps.[14]

An earlier notation indicates that murder in Dorset Street was not an unusual occurrence:

229

Then he took me through Wentworth St. to see the Jews marketing for their Sabbath. Very little crowd. Then into Dorset Street . . . '3 stabbing cases and one murder from this street in the last 3 months'. Common lodging houses for both sexes. Where they do not ask for your marriage certificate! One very fat lady at a window. She has sat there for years. She is now too fat to get out of the door! [*sic*][15]

In contrast with the dark, dirty back alley where Mary Jane Kelly's body was found, on Commercial Street on a Saturday night you might find people on their way to the numerous pubs in the vicinity, or promenading Jewish couples on their way to the local Yiddish theatres. Indeed, the *Jewish Chronicle* of 6 January 1888 states that 'a successful "Promenade Concert" was given at the Jewish Working Men's Club, Great Alie Street on the previous evening' as well as a 'Concert for the Poor' at the Jews' Free School, just to the west of Dorset Street.

Another source of social/spatial situation in the area is the map of *Jewish east London*, which appears in the book by Charles Russell and Harry S. Lewis, *The Jew in London* (1900) (PLATE 12). This was published in response to the large-scale Jewish immigration to the East End from the 1880s onwards. It captures a complex statistical picture of the Jews' pattern of settlement at the time, showing their spread along the main roads and the streets adjacent to these, while certain areas had remained completely empty of the newcomers. Although it covers the period five to ten years after the murders, the map provides us with an interesting picture of the degree of intermingling of poor Jew and Gentile on the streets of the area. The map was able to demonstrate the true nature of the imagined 'ghetto' that had caused such consternation at the time.

We see from the map that Dorset Street (coloured dark red) had fewer than 5 per cent Jews, while streets parallel to it (coloured dark blue) had close to 100 per cent – this considerable separation of groups at the domestic scale was described by David Englander:

> The assertion of Jewish territoriality was contested street by street by an indigenous population that was alarmed by the inflationary influx on rented accommodation . . . In streets colonized by Jewish and Irish immigrants tensions ran high. Thus Duke Street and Black Lion Yard, with their mixed populations, were both considered dangerous . . . The trend, though, was towards complete segregation at the residential scale; streets tended 'to become all Jewish or remain all English'.[16]

In a walk round a district 'bounded on the North by Quaker St., on the East by Brick Lane, Old Montague St. & Vallance Rd (Late Baker's Row) on the South by White-chapel High St. & on the West by Commercial Street, being part of the parishes of Christchurch Spitalfields & St. Mary's Whitechapel', the Booth notebooks state: 'This is the last of an Irish colony: the Jews begin to predominate when Grey Eagle street is reached.'

This separation continued in religious and social activity. Another authority, Judy Glasman, shows that the small synagogues known as *stieblach* were frequently located in adapted rooms or buildings which underwent a temporary change of function created by setting up the necessary furniture required for prayer. In addition to their religious function, the *stieblach* were used to organise the collection of dues for payment in the case of sickness, temporary incapacity and old age. In some of these cases, as was the Eastern European practice, the congregants of one synagogue might be made up of members of the same trade. As shown by Anne Kershen, grouping by trade led to grouping by trade union.[17] So even though religious observance was less widespread than in the old country, this did not lead to Jewish immigrants stopping

A group of East End men and boys, *c.*1900
The man reading the Daily Chronicle, *a radical daily newspaper, is more smartly dressed than*
those around him. The worn and ragged clothing, a frayed cuff here and a missing button there,
suggests a degree of poverty amongst the bystanders. The premises behind is a billiard hall.
Bagatelle, a form of bar-billiards, was a popular pastime in London in the late nineteenth
century and Burroughs & Watts made the special tables.

their attendance at a synagogue, as it served both as a source of their social network and as an economic support structure. This is illustrated by the map of churches, schools and pubs, which shows the close juxtaposition of the churches and synagogues of the area, but often separated by a street (PLATE 11).

*

232

The 1891 census provides more information on the population mix in the vicinity of the murder locations.[18] Of the 372 inhabitants in Dorset Street, 42 per cent of Jewish workers for whom there is an occupation listed were in the clothing manufacturing business, and only 3 per cent of their non-Jewish neighbours were classified as such. In contrast, the most common occupations for the non-Jewish inhabitants were: carman (large-vehicle driver who moved furniture or large goods, 5 per cent), docker (dock worker who loaded and unloaded cargo, 13 per cent), hawker (9 per cent) and labourer (10 per cent); and almost none of their Jewish neighbours did these jobs. It is clear that there was little common ground between the two immigrant groups from the point of view of industrial activity, but to what degree were the Jewish immigrants separated from their neighbours outside of work? Segregation by religion was fairly strict among the relatively prosperous, but the very poor were obliged to mix. Numerous entries in the notebooks record a mixture of Jewish and Irish in the same street and occasionally in the same dwelling: see for example the following text transcribed from the Booth notebooks:

> West along Brushfield St. North up Gun St. Very rough. Mixture of dwelling houses & factories. 3 st[orey] & attic houses. A Jewish common lodging at the N.W. end. Where the Jew thieves congregate. It is called 'the poor Jews home' on the board outside. South of Brushfield St. Gun Lane is rougher than the North end. Street narrow. Loft across from wall to wall. Old boots & mess in St. 4½ st[orey] houses, a lodging house at S.E. end. Dilapidated looking: ticket of leave men living here: at least dark blue on map purple. 'But it is not a street particularly noted for prostitutes!' at the North end is Fort St. Fairly well to do. Pink rather than purple of map: 'Jew middlemen live here' – it is Steward St. 4 storied. Windows dirty but pink in map purple. Duke St. has houses on East side. The west side is all factories &

warehouses. Character d[ark] blue to [light blue] in [1888] map purple. The coster flower & fruit sellers in Liverpool St. come from here! Inhabitants are a mixture of Jews & Irish. South into Artillery Lane. 3 st[orey] synagogue on West side.[19]

Returning to the space syntax maps we see that there were quite well integrated streets very close to the more segregated back alleys. What does this tell us about the character of the East End's local streets? Previous research has shown that the spatial form of the city sets in motion the process by which collections of buildings become the living cities we know, with all their density and diversity of spaces and activities. Studies of cities around the world have found that the layout of the urban grid shapes movement flows, so that some locations in the grid are naturally movement-rich, while others are naturally movement-poor. The consequence for places like the East End is that although the different class and religious groups might be separated at the residential scale (in the back streets) once they were in the busy main roads they were not only 'co-present' – the basic ingredient of community – but also had the potential for social interaction, at the very least through trade and industry.

CONCLUSIONS

Prior to 1888, piecemeal slum clearances had taken place in the East End and elsewhere in London. These had no more than a localised effect, and in fact in some areas overcrowding and concentration of poverty was exacerbated by the clearance of adjacent neighbourhoods. This caused the closed, crooked courts to fill up with the

☞   The London County Council's Boundary Street estate
Photograph by Mike Seaborne, 2001.

most impoverished of the people from the district that had been cleared. Following the publication of Booth's maps (and the Ripper murders themselves), there was increasing public pressure to clear out the poor areas and tidy up the existing 'almost endless intricacy of courts and yards crossing each other . . . like a rabbit warren' (as described by Henry Mayhew in *London Labour and the London Poor*). Robin Evans has since commented that the reason for the campaign to destroy poor areas in the nineteenth century was that they were viewed by the public as breeding grounds for indecency. Overcrowding was linked with immorality. The morphology – the physical form and layout of the city – was *itself* viewed by the general public as a source of the immorality of its inhabitants, and was considered a significant obstacle to policing.[20] Booth's maps were able to lift the curtain of image and stereotypes and to create an informed basis for new legislation to alleviate the situation of the East End. As shown by Bill Fishman, following the Ripper murders two Acts of Parliament were passed that were to have a profound effect on the living conditions of the East End: the Housing of the Working Classes Act 1890, which enabled local authorities to purchase land for improvement schemes, and the Public Health Amendment Act 1890, which empowered every urban authority to make by-laws regarding supply of water to WCs, paving of yards and other aspects of sanitation. Under this Act, unhealthy areas could be reported to the local authority on the grounds that any houses, courts or alleys were unfit for human habitation due to their narrowness, closeness, bad arrangement or the bad condition of streets and houses. Rather than overcrowding, urban layout – the morphology *itself* – had been identified as the source of urban degeneration.

By the end of the nineteenth century a number of Building Acts were passed in order to transform the traditional London morphology. These Acts stipulated minimum street widths, maximum ratio of height to street width, no courts, no entrances closed off from the streets and no dead-end streets. These rules resulted in building at higher densities, with greater distance between the blocks than before. Instead of building dense aggregations of two-storey houses arranged in courts and alleys, housing was constructed with a set-back from the road in front of the block to cope with the new height requirements, and with open space between the blocks at the rear. The spacing restrictions also prevented infill development. Height limits meant more restrictions on building proximity (due to the need for air circulation).

Regulations also governed the form of staircase and balcony access. Although balconies were highly valued by tenants, they were viewed as enabling an unhealthy mixing of people within a block. Finally, legislation was increasingly passed on rooms and their layout – minimum sizes were laid out and houses were ideally to be self-contained. For the first time legislation explicitly defined the ways the buildings could be arranged and guaranteed that in the future there were to be no more complicated arrangements of rooms without outside access, light and air.

All of these Acts together were seen as solving the problem of the poor – as to safeguarding health, reforming morals and ensuring supervision. In addition they were planned to eliminate close association and high density, which were thought to be undesirable in the working classes. Thus began the end of philanthropic housing and the start of municipal and government-led housing provision. If the labyrinth ever truly existed in 1888, it was soon to be straightened out by legislation, and the process of dispersing the poorest classes to the suburbs was to be set in motion. Jerry White sums this up succinctly:

Within six years Jack the Ripper had done more to destroy the Flower and Dean Street rookery than fifty years of road building, slum clearance and unabated pressure from the police, Poor Law Guardians, Vestries and Sanitary Officers.[21]

238

CHAPTER SEVEN

JACK THE RIPPER –
A LEGACY IN PICTURES

CLIVE BLOOM

THE EAST END

The East End is both a geographical location and a location for filmic fantasy. It is a space where historical circumstance gives rise to imaginative hallucinations which may be turned into celluloid dreams. Thus the East End of London becomes at once truncated into the 'East End' and that in turn is truncated into a cobbled street, a blind alley, a gaslit corner. The real and the tangible of history become the fractured scenario of nostalgia *for* history, a ruined memory of a landscape now reduced to its significant effects, glimpses of a lost place that never quite existed.

Precisely because this is a space that never quite existed it can be turned into a fantasy scene where film-makers can elaborate on the tropes of the 'East End', just as one imagines 'Ruritania' or Dracula's Gothic castle in Transylvania or the prim world

By the early twentieth century, the Ripper had metamorphosed into a Freudian nightmare. Given the Surrealists' interest in Freud and dreams it is not surprising that psychotic murderers should surface in the art of the period. In Max Ernst's 'visual' novel, Une Semaine de Bonté (1934), *which was fashioned out of a collage of found Victorian illustrations, the image becomes a subliminal recording of primal phallic fright: the bird's beak, the foot and the knife being classic Freudian sexual symbols.*

239

of Poirot. The prevailing moods of the East End are alternatively terror and paranoia, so that to enter this world is immediately to anticipate the thrill of these two emotions. People do not live in the East End of the film world so much as 'creep' and 'cower'. Night-time spells danger, and the working class become a slum peasantry whispering incantations of protection on their way home from the pub and defending themselves behind locked doors. The devil is abroad ... but garlic won't save you this time.

Here it is always 1888 and things are inevitably repeated as they must be repeated, for this East End and this story have given rise to a genre in film and literature – and expectations are set at the very beginning. The genre was established in the shadow-filled world of the silent movies, in Britain, America and Germany, and its essential elements were retained in *Waxworks* (1924); *The Lodger* (1926); *Pandora's Box* (1929); *The Phantom Fiend* (1935); *Room to Let* (1949); *The Man in the Attic* (1954); *Jack the Ripper* (1958 and 1959); *Yours Truly, Jack the Ripper* (1961); *A Study in Terror* (1965); *Knife in the Darkness* (1968); *The Ruling Class* (1968); *Hands of the Ripper* (1971); *Jack the Ripper* (1976); *Murder by Decree* (1979); *Time after Time* (1979); *Jack the Ripper* (1988) and *From Hell* (2001).

Such films require a landscape which is as real and as powerful as the East End that is depicted, but it must be cleared of ambiguity and the detritus of history if it is to become a place in the mind and moreover a scene for imaginative play. Thus the look of the place becomes vital for the primal scene of murder which is the *raison d'être* of such movies. The scene must enhance the frisson of horror. An 'East End' of the mind is the scene of terror and nothing must detract from that effect; everything must be mysterious, half glimpsed, half acknowledged. It is endless night in the East End of the mind.

This is why the fictional East End is rarely if ever shot on location, because this world has to be isolated and contained, its alleys and cobbled ways an equivalent

In John Brahm's The Lodger *(1944) there are murky fog, gas lamps and endless brick walls — all signifying the filmic 'East End'. Note also the claustrophobic atmosphere produced by a built set.*

to the labyrinths of the mind, endlessly uncoiling, but endlessly confined in a circumscribed place. The East End has to be recreated in filmland as a set, so that it is airless, claustrophobic and without escape or egress; there is no sky, nothing indicates an outside world. Water may lap by the banks of the Thames, yet it is oily, going

⬁ One of Eddie Campbell's scratchy and edgy illustration pages from the graphic novel From Hell *(1989). Here the Ripper is about to kill Mary Kelly, the whole set of events given its full weight of horror in the sequence of black and white full-page illustrations that accompany the text.*

Another illustration by Eddie Campbell with the Ripper shown standing over Mary Kelly's body, but now transported to the contemporary surroundings of the office block built over the site of the killing. The picture clearly illustrates the uncanny gap between historical memory and present-day oblivion.

nowhere, lapping simply for effect. Everything is an effect to lead us to the scene, *that* scene we have nervously half avoided and yet anticipated, expected, waiting for the rush of adrenalin when Jack appears, when Jack finally strikes and the set constructed around his absence finally reveals the reason for its construction.

Such a landscape, with its half-glimpsed doorways and foggy passages, its blind walls and relentless dull brick exteriors, which somehow leads down to the wharves and

A crowd gathers, a still from The Lodger *(1926). The crowd was a new and disturbing phenomenon in the nineteenth century. An East End crowd only gathers in movies to signify trouble and hysteria.*

A crowd gawks at the body of a victim in Doctor Jekyll and Sister Hyde *(1971)*.

docks of the Thames, becomes the equivalent of the grand Gothic of the nineteenth-century imagination, rethought and reconvened in the heart of the city as an unknown and unknowable space of dread, filled with half-perceived nightmare images. It is a Piranesi landscape where brick walls and cobbles are the equivalent of the Gothic dungeon and torture chamber; the charnel house has become the modern morgue.

This world is not empty, for it teems with life, but life that has gone to the bad. It is a world of diseased skin and cracked and toothless smiles. The inhabitants are forever coming out of the 'boozer', drunk and arm in arm, or out of the pawnshop or hanging around street corners smoking in the shadows, up to no good. Ragged

The film poster for The Lodger *(1926) is a superb art deco rendition of the Ripper in the shadows. The film's subtitle* A Story of the London Fog *gives in words the atmosphere usually offered in images. There was no fog in the autumn of 1888 when the murders took place, but fog is a trope of the film versions of Jack the Ripper.*

children lurk in dirty and torn clothes, and inebriated women looking for their rent stroll in cheap feather boas and red petticoats saying (with a wink) 'Sixpence, guv'nor' or 'Cheers, duck', for this world has its own patois. Sailors skulk and the whores half-heartedly solicit until Jack catches their fated eye. It is a world full of stereotypes.

History therefore has to be turned into a pastiche so that it too may act as a trope

Georg Pabst's masterpiece, Pandora's Box *(1929), saw the use of one of the German Expressionists' great innovations – that of light and shadow, which turned the tale of the Ripper from one which was linear and literary to one which was dominated by the visual. Here Lulu, played by Louise Brooks, is about to meet her end at the hands of Dr Schön (aka Jack the Ripper), played by Franz Lederer.*

of itself. The problem is how to 'recreate' the 1880s with sufficient information but without the messy actuality. History must become other than itself and conform to a narrative order that it never had at the time. True history has no neat storyline with a beginning, middle or end, nor a convenient denouement to leave the audience happy. The true history of Jack the Ripper is one of frustration, because the story has no closure. It is a tale full of a hopelessness that has led criminologists and historians, storytellers, quacks and fraudsters, and those looking for a quick buck, to *claim* the solution – the final solution – that only a fiction may offer. History and film are therefore antithetical, aiming as they do at different ends by different means. History provides the raw material of film, and film provides a psychic geography for audiences to play within; history is linear, film is spatial, requiring a look and a concrete place for action.

The filmic is a place for instant identifications: we need that pang of recognition. Like the story of Robin Hood, the tale of Jack the Ripper has stepped out of history and into legend, and film deals only in the legendary, and the legendary has a format and a plot which are unambiguous, and which the audience can identify and recognise. The murdered women all named and in order, the morgue, the faceless killer exposed at the end, the ubiquitous brothel scene, the bumbling police and the flashing knife. It is the scene that sets the tone for the whole show. What is a Jack the Ripper film without the imagined East End? Just another slasher movie.

THE RIPPER

The mass fascinated Edgar Allan Poe, who wrote a short story which traces the perambulations of a nameless and faceless individual whose very nature delineates him as a symbol of the vicious. It is no accident that the story is called *The Man of the Crowd*. Poe's character is a man hiding a wicked secret never to be discovered within the crowd itself, all individuality lost.

The Ripper is part of the crowd but not of it. The throng that fills the boulevards in the West End, visiting bookshops and cafés, walking its pampered pets, the throng that may be found at the races (in *My Fair Lady*) or in the department store (in *Gigi*) dressed in the height of fashion, is not the East End crowd. The East End crowd gathers furtively at street corners and fills the spaces in front of a yard or warehouse

A woman menaced by a top hat, a still from From Hell *(2001). The Ripper's shadow precedes him and has an almost preternatural life of its own. Once the shadow falls there is no escape.*

where a body has been found. It cranes its collective neck to get a better look until a policeman parts it and sends it on its collective way. The crowd here is a trope for trouble and it gathers at moments of disturbance or uncertainty. It is this crowd which becomes the mob, a vigilante force – seen in a hundred horror movies – marching to the castle with lighted torches. Here it is patrolling the misty streets or pushing into mortuaries or being silenced by judge or coroner when something juicy is mentioned in court: always it is hysterical, bigoted and nasty.

The crowd profoundly disturbed the nineteenth-century onlooker. It also gave rise to its own species, the *flâneur* or gentleman idler, strolling unseen along the avenue intent on no good. Jack is the *flâneur*, in dress and demeanour, but he crosses

over to the East End. The Ripper is the link between West End elegance and East End squalor. Indeed, in film he is the *only* link between the two sides of the metropolis.

Jack emerges through the gloom, framed in a doorway or under a street light, a pea-souper fog swirling around him. To invite him over the threshold is death. Yet he enters, with his long coat, face-masking scarf and medical bag, a bag he never lets go. In the silent era, he wears modern clothes, usually topped by a trilby. The historical events are near enough to need no costume. But by the 1960s he is dressed as a gentleman should be in evening wear, cloak and top hat. He is now the symbol of predatory aristocracy, and that is how he must remain, wrapped in the mystery of money and opulence, slumming in the East End. For at least a decade before Stephen Knight's *Jack the Ripper: The Final Solution* (1976) there was no possibility of undoing the powerful mixture of royal connivance and Masonic intrigue that Knight seemed to confirm in his work.

For the Ripper had found his most powerful ally in the monarchy. No longer a marginal and deranged basket case, he was now at the heart of the establishment, and if Walter Sickert and the Duke of Clarence could be dragged in so much the better for the story. From the 1960s, the fiction of Jack the Ripper took on the look of a Grimms' tale, shaping itself into a morality play for modernity and a powerful critique of the establishment. People had ceased to trust authority and Jack reflected this trend. For the most part, the establishment played the part of the villain while the working class, throughout, remained exploited and put-upon. How then could Jack be one of the working class? Jack had to be an aristocrat, a reprise of the penny-dreadful villains of the 1840s who hovered over half-fainting virgins.

His ubiquitous cloak envelops his victim like the cloak of Dracula, and the

Jack's handiwork is captured in From Hell *(2001). The mysterious man in the cloak leaves another victim sprawled on the ground.*

Ripper becomes a vampire, but this time a vampire who throws a shadow. And what a shadow. A play of light and shade only, nevertheless this is part of the 'founding myth of the Ripper' and has nothing to do with historical fact, but everything to do with narrative and film and filmic atmosphere. It becomes part of the Ripper's persona, but detached, an independent witness to evil. Indeed, by such accretions the myth begins. The shadow crawls up walls, round corners and across streets. The Ripper is always backlit, his shadow is always the stupendous dark double that creeps by his side or precedes him. The pull of the mythic was too strong to escape. And when his tale took on the strange resonance of a royal conspiracy theory, it became glamorous, an attractive and alluring puzzle, and no longer a mere story of murder.

The identity of the Ripper is at first symbolic. He carries a medical bag, he carries a knife – long, thin and surgical. The Ripper has long been associated with medicine whether as a surgeon, midwife or abortionist. His knife stabs, cuts and rips, implying both precision and butchery. The knife and its wounds give the Ripper's case its ambiguity and air of intrigue. How can a knife be both precise and a tool of butchery? The knife blade must be seen to enter and it must withdraw covered in blood. It is not merely the obligatory phallic substitute but the instrument of punishment for the phallic drive. As such, the substitute intercourse represented by the knife thrust must be erotic and repellent. Where the blood spurts is all important: a cum shot of death which leaves the killer cold and distant. Only after he realises his actions does he run, for there is little time to gloat. The knife is the shiny connection between the world of the West End and that of the East. It shines and reflects even in the dark. In the knife is reflected the face of the victim. The weapon itself seems uncannily to have a memory.

The Ripper as a doctor is the longest and most potent idea in the canon of Ripper beliefs. It poses the insidious with the benevolent, and makes him twice as creepy. The doctor who is a killer, a bad and by definition mad physician, is a favourite of the genre and the Ripper can join Dr Frankenstein, Dr Jekyll, Dr Fu Manchu, Dr No, the real doctors Crippen and Shipman, the wise Dr Who and the sidekick Dr Watson in the pantheon of medical men who have been spawned since the nineteenth century. The doctor is an ambiguous figure, at one and the same time a bene-factor of mankind and a serial killer, an intimate stranger and a pervert, a professional and a butcher.

Yet there are doctors and doctors. The Ripper is no mere analogue of Robert Louis Stevenson's Dr Jekyll, even if the narrative similarities suggest as much. It is true that the idea of the double takes hold of a nineteenth century struggling with inadequate words for mental dissociation, but Dr Jekyll's schizoid nature continues to acknowledge good and evil (indeed that is his tragedy: moved by compulsions that he cannot control but that still carry the moral weight of free will and choice), while Mr Hyde is openly animalistic and brutal in front of others.

Ralph Bates looks suitably menacing and psychotic in Doctor Jekyll and Sister Hyde *(1971), as he plays with his knife in the shadows while trying out Dr Jekyll's top hat. The film adds the doppelgänger theme and thus combines two cinema genres.*

The Ripper is closer to the film version of Victor Frankenstein. This is especially so in the Hammer remake of the Universal classic of 1957. In *The Curse of Frankenstein* we have an increasingly obsessed Victor – armed with medical bag and knife, and dressed in top hat and cloak in the peculiar contemporary costume Victoriana so beloved of Hammer – who goes out at night or on secret missions to retrieve body parts of the dead (recall the Ripper legend – the dismembering of the victims, the hunt for the uterus, the eaten kidney) in order to build his schizoid double, who turns monstrous because of the substitution of a mad brain. Both Victor

The Lodger (1926) has the supposed 'Avenger' or Jack the Ripper figure emerge through the fog that always accompanies him. In this scene, he stands on the doorstep and is about to be welcomed in unsuspectingly, a feature of myths surrounding the devil.

and the Monster are mad, but Victor locked in his laboratory and driven by the passion that will sacrifice the women of his household is maddest of all.

Jack was the 'monster' of the nineteenth century, but he soon became the homicidal maniac of the 1930s, 1940s and 1950s, the psychopath of the 1960s and 1970s, and the serial killer of the late twentieth century. He changes his nomenclature for every decade, giving rise to both Norman Bates with his mother fixation, and Hannibal Lecter with his taste for human flesh. In this respect the Ripper has given life to both a type and a genre beyond the immediate surroundings of his crime. He has provided a script which killers and film-makers have followed ever since. The lone, psychologically deranged killer becomes the symbol for existential fear and self-loathing. He is Georg Pabst's final vision of destruction in *Pandora's Box* (1928), Fritz Lang's warning of fascism in *M* (1931) and Alfred Hitchcock's sense of beatnik destructiveness in *Pycho* (1960).

The police, meanwhile, are flatfoots, incompetents; their accents betray their working-class origins. Here are the uniformed branch with their capes and helmets, truncheons and lanterns patrolling the dark and dangerous streets, the audience anticipating the shock of discovery and the nostalgic alarm of the police whistle which brings help to the scene. Here too is Scotland Yard, filled with those plainclothes, lumpen hacks who feature only in detective fiction from Sherlock Holmes to Agatha Christie and who touch their forelocks or wring their hats in the presence of a gentleman. They are here sweating into their tweed coats, looking puzzled over claptrap forensics, being queasy at the morgue, scratching their heads, smoking copious pipes and cigarettes, forever using old-fashioned phones, working all night, drinking cups of tea and calling colleagues into their dingy, chaotic offices. Of course there is the Commissioner demanding results, and poor Abberline or his equivalent taking the flak, but finally coming up trumps, against the odds and on a hunch that no one else would believe. Always in Scotland Yard are the men who can't see what's under their noses (although it never quite is). The ordinary police are never represented as competent or efficient in Ripper movies and the 'authenticity' accorded the working class in British socialist realist films merely evaporates. Who could expect the working class to defeat their sophisticated and devious aristocratic adversary?

The Ripper is marked out from the beginning as extraordinary. His crimes are *the* crimes, definitive because grand and squalid at the same time, bizarre and macabre in their execution. How then can anyone except someone with extraordinary attributes catch him? In *Time after Time* (1979) he is chased across time and space by H. G.

Wells, the Ripper having learned the secrets of time travel. In the comic book *Gotham by Gaslight*, published in 1989, the auspicious year that Alan Moore and Eddie Campbell's graphic novel *From Hell* also appeared, Batman himself is transplanted into a Victorian New York where the Ripper is no less than the man who murdered Bruce Wayne's parents. There's a symbiotic relationship with the caped crusader, and the myths of Batman and the Ripper merge, one imaginary and one real, both dark, Gothic, on the brink of psychosis, disguised and schizoid, the one becoming the other. The mirroring of their stories is caught in the repetition compulsion of the primal act, endlessly needing to be retold, a point made explicit in the opening 'letter' by Robert Bloch to the readers of *Gotham by Gaslight*.

We are fascinated with 'what if' scenarios. If the Ripper defeats us in real life, he cannot elude us in fiction. So what better adversary than Jack's near contemporary, Sherlock Holmes? Indeed the merest hint of a deerstalker glimpsed by a witness is the key to the famous detective's filmic head apparel in both illustration and film. Holmes is the *flâneur*, forensic expert, consulting detective and genius who alone can face the Ripper.

In *The Hound of the Baskervilles* (1902), we meet two versions of the Ripper. One is Selden, the Notting Hill murderer, just escaped on to Grimpen Mire from Princetown Prison, a man who had committed a crime filled with 'peculiar ferocity' and 'wanton brutality'; he only escaped the hangman's noose due to 'doubts as to his complete sanity, so atrocious was his conduct'. The musing is Watson's, but Holmes has the scent of another candidate, the vicious and sadistic Stapleton who masquerades in London as the detective himself, telling cabbies his name is Holmes; the Ripper as doppelgänger of his nemesis. No wonder Holmes tells Watson that

Batman to the rescue! In the comic book Gotham by Gaslight *(1989) Batman comes face to face with Jack the Ripper in New York City. In this sequence the Ripper's hansom cab is drawn by the horses of the apocalypse.*

256

they have 'a foeman who is worthy of [their] steel'. For the moment, Holmes is 'checkmated in London'. Only in 'the fantastic landscape of a dream', transported as he is to Devonshire and Baskerville Hall, can Holmes work his magic. He works this magic entirely without police help, for the Ripper is the perfect foil for the fictional detective or the amateur sleuth in all of us.

What the detective detects however is not crime, for the Ripper goes a considerable way beyond mere murder – and film directors, story-makers and 'Ripperologists' know it. Instead the Ripper initiates an existential quest for the origin of meaning. He is the avenging God in a godless world, and philosophers of the human condition such as Sherlock Holmes and Sigmund Freud are his only worthy opponents. This is still, nevertheless, a police story as long as the Scotland Yard detective is of a philosophical bent.

By a paradox the fictional police do finally defeat the Ripper, creating a satisfying narrative closure that was denied them in reality, for the whole point of fiction is to name what could not be named in history, and to bring the Ripper to the justice he escaped all those years ago. The job of the police in such narratives is to act as society's moral guardian, and what starts as a criminal investigation soon becomes an exploration of corruption: either aristocracy's parasitism, or a high-level Masonic conspiracy, or the mad plans of a psychopath whose daytime respectability hides his perverted sexual tastes and in which the final scene produces the exposure and removal of that corruption. The police are charged with putting a face on the Ripper, a face only his victims and the audience have glimpsed. It is not the face alone, but the eyes that designate the perversity and personal corruption of the Ripper: he must have mad eyes, for the police have to arrest not merely a horrible person but a person 'from Hell'.

There is always a supernatural element to the investigation of the Ripper murders, and 'ghost walks' still people the East End with the Ripper's victims. He is still invoked in modern-day violence against women ('the Yorkshire Ripper' (1975–80); 'the

Ipswich Ripper' (2006)), and he walks the corridors (at least in fiction) of the office blocks that are now built on the site of his crimes. The police arrest a ghost, but a ghost that won't be laid, a revenant ready to rise up in innumerable fictional and filmic sequels, to return as a zombie lord in Hirohiko Araki's epic *JoJo's Bizarre Adventure* (begun in 1984), to be pursued across time and space by H. G. Wells, defeated by Sherlock Holmes or hunted down by Batman.

In Nicholas Meyer's Time after Time *(1979) H. G. Wells played by Malcolm McDowell pursues the Ripper across time. This is another version of the cross-over genre which keeps the Ripper alive in the movies. Here, David Warner (the Ripper) gets to grips with a calculator.*

Rippers are the missing place on the map. They (for there are many now) represent a dark space that has to be lit and given a face. The Ripper was the first transatlantic celebrity, as well known in America as in the British Empire itself, a favourite of the newspapers, a sensation whose exploits were immediately copied in the teeming streets of New York, Baltimore and Chicago: a true son of the mid-Atlantic.

The Ripper broods over modernity. His crimes represent a new aesthetic, the aesthetic of the ugly to be found in the work of the Surrealists and in Dada, influenced by the explorations of Freud. The beautiful in art was already out of date in the 1880s when the Belgian symbolists came to London; Whistler was howled down by Ruskin and the public. A new aesthetic dispensation was abroad and the decay and decadence which seemed to follow the Ripper was in accord with the rise of magic, Satanism, absinthe and green carnations that marked the end of century.

The Ripper is a figure from the modernist canon, where 'the desolate cosmos' seems all there is after Auschwitz and Hiroshima, and where the mental universe is obsessed with its own destruction or abjection. As a cultural icon the Ripper is just as at home in the work of the modernist composer Alban Berg where he appears in the third act of the opera *Lulu* (1931; performed 1937) as on the sleeve of Screaming Lord Sutch's 1972 rock album, *The Hands of the Ripper*.

He fascinates us still in an age of voyeurism and existential angst, where slippage, the subversive and the borderline take centre stage. The Ripper is also postmodern for, from being 'culturally marginal', the 'deviant' has been repositioned as an exemplar of 'radical, transgressive sexuality'. 'Perverted longings are not merely to be dismissed as individual aberrations but may reveal in concentrated form important underlying structures affecting the behaviour of whole societies.' The image of the Ripper will endure as long as these paradigms endure. As in London so in Tokyo. A Japanese punk band even has his name and he appears in Japanese violent 'pink' movies such as *Assault, Jack the Ripper!* (*Boko Kirisaki Jakku*, 1976), a pornographic orgy of relentless erotic horror and violence.

THE WOMEN

The Ripper murdered women. In itself this is neither entertaining nor pleasant, but in film and imagination the women become types in a catalogue like Henry VIII's wives. Historians have tried to humanise the Ripper's victims, give them a life, recreate their backgrounds and complex relationships. But they remain ciphers for the murderer; inevitably, they will meet their fate. We cannot invest much interest in those who are mere adjuncts, appendages to the Ripper, those whose fate is already sealed with their first appearance on screen. Like the brides of Dracula, these women are somehow both victims and marriage partners – love and death at first sight. They exist to scream and die. The sordid, 'real-world' circumstances of 'knee tremblers' down dark and putrid alleys, or the regularity of anal intercourse against paint-peeled doorways with women who were both ill fed and ill kempt, and whose looks suggest the worst excesses of the anorexic, are not likely to appeal either to film audiences or casting directors. How can a film star look like a half-starved streetwalker? Actresses who portray prostitutes are keyed to a different look, and this is the voluptuous. Figures are full, curves are plentiful and bosoms overflow; the corset is much in evidence, as are stockings and negligées. There must be much display of the erotic potential of all this corsetry, all this peek-a-boo sexuality. Inevitably this leads the viewer not to a back doorstep, but to the brothel where much is made of breasts and legs, of hints and tantalising

An illustration from Thomas Peckett Prest's Varney the Vampire or The Feast of Blood *(a serial which ran for two years between 1845 and 1847), one of the first great penny-dreadful shockers. Here with voluminous cloak and cowering virgin are almost all the ingredients of the Ripper myth in imagery.*

glimpses; champagne flows. Later we will visit the alehouse where gin-soaked drunks will paw the breasts of drunken wenches (as if this was an eighteenth-century romp) amid much laughter, smoke and noise, all of which give the story an erotics that is sadly missing from the emaciated and ageing faces of the real victims.

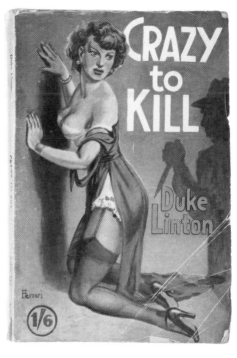

The book cover of X Esquire *(1927) by Leslie Charteris shows a woman cringing before the oversized face of the master criminal. Here the image is closer to that of a sinister murderer (something the book is not about) with its use of an old-fashioned top hat and black mask. Such images of menace were used successfully to sell such books.*

In Duke Linton's 1950s exploitation pulp novel Crazy to Kill, *the menaced woman shows 'plenty of stocking' as the shadow of the knifeman looms ever closer. Such novels, with their hints of sleaze and depravity, popular with men in the period of national service, were the British equivalent and substitute for the genuine American version by writers such as Mickey Spillane. Duke Linton's real name was Steve Frances.*

Thus the portrayal of Jack's victims becomes the greatest betrayal and the greatest divergence from historical fact. In film, Jack's women are bosomy, beautiful, flirtatious and overwhelmingly sexual. They exude the erotic potential of all fictitious prostitutes (*Lulu*; *Pretty Woman*; *Belle de Jour*): these play-acting women of the streets must exude an erotic atmosphere that will appeal to contemporary audiences. Hence their portrayal in one era is radically different in another, different from one country to the next. Nothing changes so fast as eroticism. So the actresses playing the part of nineteenth-century whores are always up-to-date in their make-up and hair styles (think of Louise Brooks or even Barbara Windsor), merely dressed in the vague costume of the 1880s which soon duplicates that of the later 'naughty' nineties with its aristocratic glamour, fun-filled sex houses, opium dens and the allure of the cancan.

Most of all, these actresses have to replace the brutal, casual sexual encounters of their real-life counterparts with the allure of dalliance with a beautiful courtesan. Films must teeter on the brink of pornography without

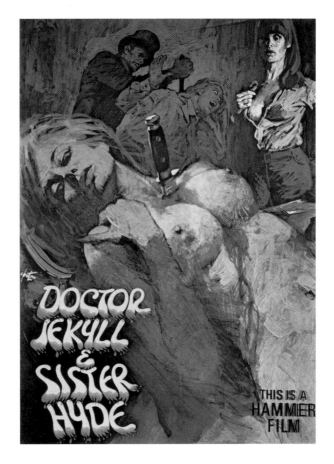

The sexual mores of the 1970s took things further than they had gone before. In the Hammer Horror film poster of Doctor Jekyll and Sister Hyde *(1971), a phallic knife sticks out of a very buxom chest. The woman looks less dead than sexually satisfied.*

becoming pornographic. On screen, the life of these women is an erotic come-on driven by the seduction of the viewer, while in the narrative this come-on is met with the phallic eroticism of Jack's knife in the final *Liebestod*.

A woman screams against those ubiquitous shadows in A Study in Terror *(1965).*
Screaming women are the trope of East End *menace. In this still, the woman manages*
to scream despite the fact that her throat has been cut!

Carolyn Seymour playing the 'working-class tart made good' does the required sexy striptease before being knifed to death by Jack the Ripper in the highly subversive The Ruling Class *(1969). The film tells the story of a schizophrenic aristocrat, played by Peter O'Toole, who begins the film as Jesus Christ and ends it as the Ripper, in a satiric look at the establishment.*

To scream and die may be what these women do, but they exist for more than that. It is through the women of the story that the 'true' East End reveals itself and it is the women who take us there. Through them we are introduced to the characters and suspects that people the story and therefore the actresses must be beautiful or we may not offer them the sympathy that takes us into their world and allows us to witness

In this publicity shot for The Hands of the Ripper *(1971), Eric Porter is caressed by actresses dressed in the obligatory boas and feathers which always signify fallen women in such films. The costumes are Victoriana rather than Victorian.*

their end. By being portrayed as erotic these actresses oddly reinstate the humanity the victims were denied in historical reality.

Shadows follow the menaced woman as she walks the street and as she climbs the stairs. Her eyes give it away as she hurries on. The menaced woman is the centre of the plot. Beguiled by the mysterious man in the hansom cab, she knows too late the net she is entangled within. Only she sees the face of the Ripper, revealed seconds before her death; only she realises (until the final climactic scene of the movie) the identity of her killer. The shadow of the knife, like the shadow of Nosferatu's claw-like hand, clutches symbolically at her breast. She is trapped, eyes wide open, before the phantom menace.

Yes, the women scream and die. What is screaming but the signifier of menace? Women scream when they discover grisly remains. Screaming alerts those around that a dreadful act has occurred, and it signifies panic. Thus screaming becomes a signifier for the terror itself, an audible corollary of the horror that exists at the heart of the East End, a horror more shocking because unseen and unexplained. The scream is the noisy witness of murder, contrasted with the eerie silence that precedes the death of the victim. The scream ties the genre of Ripper land to that of Gothic horror.

CONTRIBUTORS

PETER ACKROYD is the author of *London: the Biography* and *Thames: Sacred River* as well as numerous works of fiction, poetry and biography.

CLIVE BLOOM is Emeritus Professor of English and American Studies, Middlesex University. His books include *Violent London: 2000 Years of Riots, Gothic Horror: A Reader's Guide from Poe to King and Beyond* and *Terror Within: Terrorism and the Dream of a British Republic*.

RICHARD DENNIS is Reader in Geography at UCL. He specialises in urban geography and historical geography and is the author of *Cities in Modernity: Representations and Productions of Metropolitan Space, 1840–1930*. He also wrote the chapter on 'Modern London' in the *Cambridge Urban History of Britain*.

LOUISE A. JACKSON is a Senior Lecturer at the University of Edinburgh. Her research is concerned with histories of women and gender in modern Britain as well as policing and surveillance, crime, youth and sexuality. Her books include *Child Sexual Abuse in Victorian England* and *Women Police: Gender, Welfare and Surveillance in the Twentieth Century*.

ANNE J. KERSHEN is Barnet Shine Senior Research Fellow and Director of the Centre for the Study of Migration at Queen Mary College. She has published widely, her most recent book being *Strangers, Aliens and Asians: Huguenots, Jews and Bangladeshis in Spitalfields 1660–2000*.

JOHN MARRIOTT is Reader in History and Director of the Raphael Samuel History Centre at the University of East London. He is the author of *The Culture of Labourism* and *The Other Empire and Progress in the Colonial Imagination*.

ELLEN ROSS is Professor of History and Women's Studies at Ramapo College, New Jersey. She is the author of *Love and Toil: Motherhood in Outcast London* and *Slum Travelers: Ladies and London Poverty, 1860–1920*.

LAURA VAUGHAN is a Senior Lecturer and Director of the MSc Advanced Architectural Studies at the Bartlett, UCL and a member of the Space Syntax Laboratory. She is a specialist in the effects of the urban structure on poverty and immigrant settlement patterns.

ALEX WERNER, a senior curator at the Museum of London, has curated a number of major displays including *London Bodies* and the *World City* Galleries. His publications include *Dockland Life* and *Journeys through Victorian London*.

NOTES

CHAPTER ONE
The imaginative geography of the Whitechapel murders
Appearing between pages 31 and 63

1 Jan Bondeson, *The London Monster. Terror on the streets in 1790*, Tempus, 2005.

2 This raises some awkward questions on boundaries. Of the five 'canonical' murders only two actually took place in the parish of Whitechapel. This initially created confusion in a press struggling hard to attach convenient labels, and the murders were variously described as 'London', 'East End', 'Aldgate' and 'Whitechapel'. Here I use Whitechapel to refer to the Registration District which included Spitalfields, Mile End New Town, Goodman's Fields, Aldgate and Whitechapel.

3 John Stow, *A Survey of London, written in the Year 1598*, Alan Sutton, 1994, p. 384.

4 M. Dorothy George, *London Life in the Eighteenth Century*, Peregrine, 1966. First published in 1925 this study has not been surpassed.

5 *Middlesex Records*, cited in ibid, p. 97.

6 Ibid, pp. 91–4; John Marriott, 'The spatiality of the poor in eighteenth-century London', in Tim Hitchcock and Heather Shore (eds) *The Streets of London*, Rivers Oram, 2003.

7 George Rudé, *Hanoverian London, 1714–1808*, Secker & Warburg, 1971, pp. 186–90.

8 For a much more detailed discussion and an extensive collection of the important texts, see John Marriott and Masaie Matsumura (eds) *The Metropolitan Poor. Semi-factual accounts, 1795–1910*, 6 vols, Pickering and Chatto, 1999.

9 Henry Mayhew, *London Labour and the London Poor*, Frank Cass, 1967, Vol. 1, p. 6.

10 Ibid, p. 252.

11 Ibid, pp. 408–9.

12 Gareth Stedman Jones, *Outcast London. A study of the relationship between classes in Victorian society*, Clarendon Press, 1971, Chapter 8; William Fishman, *East End 1888*, Hanbury, 1988, Chapter 2.

13 Ibid, p. 220.

14 Charles Booth, *Life and Labour of the People in London*, Williams and Norgate, 1889, Vol. 1, p. 66.

15 Watts Phillips, *The Wild Tribes of London*, Ward & Lock, 1855, pp. 64–72.

16 John Hollingshead, *Ragged London in 1861*, Smith and Elder, 1861, p. 44.

17 George Wade, 'Israel in London. How the Hebrew lives in Whitechapel', *English Illustrated Magazine*, August 1900, p. 407.

18 Stedman Jones, *Outcast London*, especially Chapter 16.

19 *East London Advertiser*, 25 August 1888, reproduced on www.casebook.org, an invaluable source of press and other reports related to the Ripper murders upon which I have relied heavily.

20 *Star*, 1 September 1888.

21 *Evening Standard*, 1 September 1888.

22 *City Press*, 5 September 1888.
23 *Pall Mall Gazette*, 7 September 1888.
24 *Penny Illustrated Paper*, 8 September 1888.
25 *The Times*, 10 October 1888.
26 See, for example, *Daily News*, 11 September 1888.
27 *East and West Ham Gazette*, 15 September 1888.
28 *Daily News*, 26 September 1888.
29 *Star*, 1 October 1888. A Thug was popularly understood as a particular type of Indian thief who garrotted his victims, and Sicarius a Jewish 'terrorist' who fought against Roman repression.
30 Cited in Fishman, *East End 1888*, p. 53.
31 George Sims, 'Human London. II. Behind the scenes in Stepney', *London Magazine*, November 1907, p. 287.
32 *The Times*, 19 September 1888, cited in Henrietta Barnett, *Canon Barnett: His Life, Work and Friends*. John Murray, 1918, Vol. 1, pp. 303–4.
33 Ibid, p. 304.
34 'Leaves from the life of a "poor Londoner"', *Good Words*, 1885, p. 532.
35 E. Dixon, 'A Whitechapel Street', *English Illustrated Magazine*, February 1890, p. 355.
36 *Daily Mail*, 16 July 1901. The whole article and its rejoinder had been usefully transcribed for the www.casebook.org website.

CHAPTER TWO

The immigrant community of Whitechapel at the time of the Ripper murders

Appearing between pages 65 and 97

1 In the nineteenth century immigrants were most generally described as aliens, the term analogous with foreigner or stranger and one which identified incomers as outsiders. The largest number of 'outsiders' in the country at the time of the Ripper murders – with the exception of the Irish who in reality were British and occupied a 'middle place' – was the Eastern European Jewish immigrant population which increasingly became known as, and generally called, alien/s. As the terms anti-Semite and anti-Semitism were not in common use those who were opposed to the alien (Jewish) presence were known as anti-aliens and their activities and behaviour as anti-alienism.

2 Estimates vary as to the exact number of Eastern Europeans in the district. The statistics were mainly taken from the Decennial Census, but as that was only taken every ten years and returns were dependent on the accuracy of the enumerator and the presence of all members of the household it is usually assumed that the figure was higher than that officially recorded.

3 The earliest immigrants were both Sephardi (Jews from the Iberian Peninsula) and Ashkenazi (Jews from Central and Eastern Europe). By the end of the 17th century each had its own, separate, burial grounds and synagogues.

4 The name given an area of 362,000 square miles to the south and west of Russia/Russian Poland between the Baltic and the Black Sea in which Russian Jews in the 19th century were forced to live. It included Lithuania, Vilna, Volhynia, Podolia, Ukraine, Crimea, Lublin and Lodz. There were some exceptions, including merchants and industrialists who were permitted access to cities such as Moscow and St Petersburg. It should perhaps be noted that whilst the creation

of the Pale of Settlement features high on the list of Russian-Jewish disadvantages, it spread over a prosperous area and contained the important airs and trade routes of Western Russia.

5 The first 'council housing' was the Boundary estate on the edge of Spitalfields and Shoreditch, in Bethnal Green, which was opened by the London County Council in 1900.

6 The Jews' Free School was established in 1817 and by the end of the nineteenth century had become one of the most admired teaching institutions in Europe. At its location in Bell Lane it accommodated over 3,000 pupils.

7 Jewish religious law.

8 The Jewish practice of frying fish gave rise to expressions of xenophobia from the native community who disliked the smell; an example of xenophobia that we see replicated in the comments made about the cooking of curry by Asian immigrants. This aspect of anti-alienism reared its head at the Trades Union Congress Conference in 1892 when delegates were attempting to pass a resolution to stop the entry of pauper aliens – for aliens read Eastern European Jews.

9 His family wish the surname to remain anonymous.

10 This is the job description that appears in the enumerator's report for 1881.

11 Translated by the author from the original which appeared in the *Arbeiter Fraint*, 19 March 1907.

12 The last two decades of the nineteenth century were significant for the fact that social conditions such as poverty, poor housing and casual employment which had been perceived by the middle classes and government as a 'condition' now became identified as problems for which the state had to take responsibility and resolve.

13 The terms anti-Semite and anti-Semitism were very new, the use of 'anti-Semitism' to describe Jew hatred first being used in Germany in the mid-1870s. In the fervour of anti-Eastern European Jews that arose in Britain from the late 1880s, the common description of the non-nationals was 'alien', those who opposed their entry were anti-alienists and their activities described as anti-alienism.

14 The building was erected in 1743 by the Huguenot community to serve as *La Neuve Eglise* for the growing refugee Calvinist community.

CHAPTER THREE

Law, order and violence

Appearing between pages 99 and 135

1 All information relating to cases coming before Thames police court July–September 1888 derives from London Metropolitan Archives, Thames Police Court Registers, PS/TH/A/01/11 and PS/TH/A/01/12. Court registers for Worship Street have not survived for this period.

2 Montagu Williams records that at Worship Street cases involving drunkenness were usually discharged with a warning.

3 The City of London Police tended to release drunks directly from custody when sober; the Metropolitan Police brought prisoners before the police court where they were usually discharged by magistrates.

4 The East End press discussed the life stories of the 'unfortunate' women who became murder victims with far more compassion than the Fleet Street papers, a likely indicator of wider community feeling. Sympathy for Mary Jane Kelly was demonstrated by the crowd of mourners who attended her funeral procession and the wreaths donated by those who were regulars of the same public houses.

5 For these two cases see *East London Observer*, 7 July 1888, and *The Times*, 14 September 1888.

6 Three cases involved alleged assaults by sons on mothers; one involved an assault by a brother on his sister; one case involved an assault on a father; in three cases the relationship between family members is unclear.

7 *East London Observer*, 14 July and 21 July 1888.

8 These include all cases of rape, indecent assault and unlawful carnal knowledge of girls under the age of consent (sometimes referred to as 'statutory rape'). Cases collected from the

Thames police court registers were cross-referenced to newspaper coverage and, if committed for trial, to the records of higher courts.

9 In 29 per cent of cases the age of the victim is not indicated.

10 The case can be followed in *The Times*, 30 November 1865 and 7 December 1865.

11 *East London Observer*, 15 May 1880.

12 *East London Observer*, 16 September 1870.

13 London Metropolitan Archives, Middlesex Sessions, Depositions, MJ/SPE/1870/08, No. 7.

14 *East London Observer*, 28 August 1885.

15 *The Times*, 14 August 1888.

16 Rebecca Bush, who took on casual work as a tailoress, was accused of theft after pawning four pairs of trousers that she was supposed to be making up 'to pay the rent'; Mr Lushington sympathetically adjourned the case for a month to give her time to redeem them. See *The Times*, 15 August 1888.

CHAPTER FOUR

Common lodgings and 'furnished rooms': housing in 1880s Whitechapel

Appearing between pages 141 and 179

1 I am grateful to Beverley Cook of the Museum of London for the details from her grand-mother's aunt's rent book (1895).

2 The census describes all these couples as 'married', but it seems unlikely that all the Dorset Street couples were legally married. Just consider the multiplicity of surnames attached to some of the Ripper's victims.

3 In the nineteenth century, when few properties were purchased for owner-occupation, the usual way of valuing property was to multiply the annual rental value by the desired profit rate, e.g.

a 5 per cent rate of return meant you would pay up to 20 times the annual rental; but if you expected, say, a 12.5 per cent return on your money, you would only be prepared to pay 8 times the rental. Basically, the more years' purchase the lower the expected or acceptable rate of return.

4 See her very valuable postings (dated 23 January 2004, 21 March 2006 and 17 July 2007) on the *Casebook: Jack the Ripper* website, www.casebook.org/index.html.

5 There were two E. Zuccanis in 1880s London:

Emilio, who lived at 108 Adelaide Road, Primrose Hill and later at 1 Prince of Wales Terrace, Kensington and died in February 1897, when he was described as 'financier'; and Ernesto, 14 Endsleigh Gardens, Bloomsbury. Their father had been a looking-glass manufacturer at 37 Skinner Street (on the west side of Bishopsgate but still only a few hundred yards from Dorset Street). By 1851 both had followed their father into the family business, Emilio living at 42 Haydon Square (south of Aldgate High Street) from where he moved round the corner to 17 Mansell Street by 1861, and Ernesto living at 4 Church Street, Whitechapel (very close to his business address, 40 Brick Lane – between Heneage and Booth Streets, where his business was still listed in 1884). Ernesto was listed in *The Times* as bankrupt in 1891 and died at 52 Highbury Park, aged 79, in 1899. On the evidence of geographical proximity, he is more likely to have been the owner of the Spitalfields property. But whichever it was, the pattern was the same: growing up in the East End as skilled craftsmen, then moving west as respected members of the London business community.

6 Ritchie's and Rowe's accounts are both reproduced in the online 'Dictionary of Victorian London': www.victorianlondon.org. Hoare's experiment is reported in Gerry Nixon, 'An East End Lodging House in the 1880s', *Ripperologist* 22 (April 1999), republished at www.casebook.org/dissertations/rip-lodginghouse.html.

7 All these cases can be followed in the pages of *The Times* (13 March 1877, 2 October 1877, 17 January 1889, 12 June 1890).

8 *Evening News*, 3 October 1888, *Star*, 12 October 1888, and *The Times*, 13 October 1888.

9 *The Times* (6 October 1882 and 30 November 1886).

10 *The Times* (17 September 1879 and 19 August 1882).

11 In January 1891 there were 144 men, 99 women and 22 children (aged less than 16) in the Refuge.

12 These figures exaggerate the number of lodging-houses by counting separately each street address where, in practice, one large lodging-house extended through several adjacent houses. Thus, in Dorset Street, fourteen registered houses comprised what were recognised on maps and by their owners as only five separate establishments.

CHAPTER FIVE

'Deeds of heroism': Whitechapel's ladies

Appearing between pages 181 and 217

1 Bill Fishman, *East End 1888*, Duckworth 1988, pp. 211–12; Philip Sugden, *The Complete History of Jack the Ripper*, Carroll & Graf Publishers, Inc., 1994, p. 127; L. Perry Curtis, *Jack the Ripper and the London Press*, Yale University Press, 2001, p. 247, and Tom Cullen, *Autumn of Terror: Jack the Ripper, His Crimes and Times*, The Bodley Head, 1965, p. 138.

2 Thomas J. Barnardo's letter to the editor, *The Times*, 9 October 1888; *Star*, 9 October 1888, p. 3; Judith R. Walkowitz, *City of Dreadful Delight: Narratives of Sexual Danger in Late-Victorian London*, University of Chicago Press, 1992, p. 222.

3 *Methodist Recorder*, 4 October 1888, p. 740; H.M., *'Twixt Aldgate Pump and Poplar. The Story*

of Fifty Years Adventure in East London, Epworth Press, 1935, p. 55. Two of these women were still on the Mission staff in 1935!

4 Quoted in Cullen, *Autumn of Terror*, p. 209; *'Twixt Aldgate Pump and Poplar*, p. 24.

5 George Holland, founder of the George Yard Mission, was one of these nervous clergymen. On Peter Thompson's statements to the press, see *The Methodist Recorder*, 4 October 1888, p. 740. See also 'An Evening in Whitechapel', *Little's Living Age*, 3 November 1888, reprinted from *Daily News*.

6 The 'matrons' proposal is in J. Jenkins, Letter to the Editor, *Evening News*, 12 November 1888, from www.casebook.org/press_reports/ evening_news/18881112.html; On Barnett's petition see Cullen, *Autumn of Terror*, pp. 136–8.

7 Beatrice Webb, *My Apprenticeship*, Cambridge University Press, 1926, p. 129; Constance Battersea, *Reminiscences*, Macmillan, 1922, Chapter 20.

8 Lydia Murdoch, *Imagined Orphans: Poor Families, Child Welfare, and Contested Citizenship in London*, Rutgers University Press, 2006, pp. 115–18.

9 Charles Booth, *Life and Labour of the People in London, Third Series: Religious Influences*, revised ed., 7 vols., McMillan, 1902, vol. II, pp. 50–53; Henry Walker, *East London: Sketches of Christian Work*, Religious Tract Society, 1896, pp. 37–47; G. Holden Pike, *Pity for the Perishing: The Power of the Bible in London*, James Clarke & Co, 1884, p. 80.

10 *'Twixt Aldgate Pump and Poplar*, p. 21; *Methodist Recorder*, 20 September 1888, p. 703; George A. Leask, *Peter Thompson: The Romance of the London Mission*, Robert Cully, n.d. p. 50; *Methodist Times*, 8 January 1891, p. 42.

11 Deborah E. Nord, *Walking the Victorian Streets: Women, Representation, and the City*, Cornell University Press, 1995, pp. 184–5.

12 Quoted in Henrietta Barnett, *Canon Barnett: His Life, Work, and Friends*, 2 vols., John Murray, 1918, vol. I, p. 105, n. 1.

13 Leonore Davidoff, 'The Origin of the Species', *Avenue Magazine*, September 1989, pp. 72–5; Carolyn Betensky, 'Philanthropy, Desire, and the Politics of Friendship in *The Princess Casamassima*', *Henry James Review*, vol. 22, 2001, pp. 147–62.

14 'Cassandra' is published as an Appendix to Ray Strachey's *'The Cause': A Short History of the Women's Movement in Great Britain*, 1928, reprint ed., Kennikat Press, n.d. The quotation is on p. 403.

15 Mary Neal, 'A Victorian Childhood', *Adelphi*, 16, new series, April 1940, pp. 285–6; Arthur Porritt, *The Best I Remember*, Cassell, 1922, p. 134.

16 Norman and Jeanne MacKenzie (eds.), *The Diary of Beatrice Webb*. Volume 1, 1873–1892, *Glitter Around and Darkness Within*, Harvard University Press, 1982, p. 132; *Methodist Times*, 2 April, 1891, p. 333.

17 Mary Neal, 'As a Tale is Told: The Autobiography of a Victorian Woman', unpublished typescript in the possession of Lucy Neal, London, p. 63.

18 Emmeline-Pethick Lawrence, *My Part in a Changing World*, Victor Gollancz, 1938, pp. 72–3.

19 Arthur Porritt, *The Best I Remember*, p. 135; Friederichs, 'I Was in Prison –', p. 304; Honnor Morten, *From a Nurse's Note-Book*, The Scientific Press, 1899, pp. 127–8.

20 MacKenzie, *The Diary of Beatrice Webb*, p. 208. Dated 13 May 1887.

21 Koven, *Slumming*, p. 184; Neal, 'As a Tale is Told', pp. 49–51; A. L. Hodson, *Letters from a Settlement*, Edward Arnold, 1909, pp. 12–15.

22 Gillian Darley, *Octavia Hill*, pp. 139, 152.

23 Henrietta Barnett, *Canon Barnett*, p. 133; Darley, *Octavia Hill*, pp. 155, 218; Carolyn Heilbrun, *The Garnett Family*, Allen & Unwin, 1961, pp. 176–7.

24 MacKenzie, *The Diary of Beatrice Webb*, pp. 41–3, March and April 1888.

25 Ibid, p. 267 (28 November); Rosemary O'Day, 'Before the Webbs: Beatrice Potter's Early Investigations for Charles Booth's Inquiry',

History 78, no. 252, February 1993, p. 233.

26 Patricia Hollis, *Ladies Elect: Women in English Local Government 1865–1914*, Clarendon Press, 1987, p. 112; Anne Taylor, *Annie Besant: A Biography*, Oxford University Press, 1992, p. 216; Shaw is quoted in Joyce Bellamy and John Saville, eds., *Dictionary of Labour Biography*, Macmillan, 1982, entry for Besant.

27 *Star*, 31 October 1888, p. 2; 9 November, p. 3; 9 October, p. 2; Taylor, *Annie Besant*, p. 217; *East London Observer*, 10 November 1888, p. 6.

28 For a different view, see Colin Clifford, *The Asquiths*, John Murray, 2002, p. 16.

29 *The Autobiography of Margot Asquith*, ed. Mark Bonham Carter, Houghton Mifflin, 1963, pp. 41, 44.

30 Liselotte Glage, *Clementina Black: A Study in Social History and Literature*, Carl Winter, 1981, pp. 30–3. *Star*, 1 November 1888, p. 2; Fishman, *East End 1888*, pp. 285–8.

31 Published under the pseudonym John Law, *Captain Lobe: A Story of the Salvation Army*, in 1889. My citations are to *In Darkest London*, a slightly later (1891) edition under the author's own name; reprint ed., Black Apollo Press, 2003, Chapter 13. The letter to the editor is quoted in Cullen, *Autumn of Terror*, p. 54. There is an excellent Harkness entry in Bellamy and Saville, *Dictionary of Labour Biography*.

32 Deborah McDonald, *Clara Collet 1860–1848: An Educated Working Woman*, Woburn Press, 2004, pp. 68–79. The sections of her 'Women's Work' article cited here are found in Booth, *Life and Labour: Poverty*, IV, pp. 257, 259, 273, 309 and 321.

33 Lynne Hapgood, '"Is this Friendship?" Eleanor Marx, Margaret Harkness and the Idea of Socialist Community', in *Eleanor Marx (1855–1898): Life, Work, Contacts*, ed. John Stokes, Ashgate, 2000, pp. 132–3, 138; Yvonne Kapp, *Eleanor Marx*, 2 vols., Pantheon Books, 1976, vol. II, pp. 280, 293, 325, 335 (quoting Engels: 'Quite an East Ender'), 361, 510, and part IV, Chapter 6.

Ellen Ross thanks James Chaffee of Ramapo College for his research assistance.

CHAPTER SIX

Mapping the East End labyrinth

Appearing between pages 219 and 237

1 Quoted in W. Fishman, *East End 1888*, 1988, p. 7.

2 See web pages written by Dr Ifan Shepherd for an extensive background to the maps: http://mubs.mdx.ac.uk/Staff/Personal_pages/Ifan1/Booth/printedmaps.htm.

3 H.J. Dyos, *Exploring the Urban Past*, Cannadine and Reeder (eds.), Cambridge University Press, 1982, pp. 140–1.

4 Gareth Stedman Jones, *Outcast London*, 1984, pp. 15–16.

5 Laura Vaughan, 'The spatial form of poverty in Charles Booth's London', in L. Vaughan (ed.) *Progress in Planning: special issue on The Syntax of Segregation*, 2007, 67, pp. 231–50. Online http://eprints.ucl.ac.uk/archive/00003273/.

6 J. A. Jackson, 'The Irish' in R. Glass (ed.), *London: Aspects of Change*, MacGibbon and Kee, Vol. 3, 1964, p. 299.

7 L. H. Lees, *Exiles of Erin: Irish migrants in Victorian London*, Manchester University Press, 1979.

8 Fishman, 1988, p. 134.

9 A. Davin, *Growing Up Poor: Home, School and Street in London 1870–1914*, Rivers Oram Press, 1996, pp. 158–9.

10 Laura Vaughan, 'The relationship between physical segregation and social marginalisation in the urban environment', *World Architecture*, 2005, pp. 185, 88–96. Online http://eprints.ucl.ac.uk/archive/00000884/.

11 It is important to note that in addition to the two immigrant populations referred to here, there was a significant population of London-born, indeed, locally born people living in the area. If we look for example at the census of 1891 for the Spitalfields district (see D. Rau, 'The 1891 Census in Spitalfields: as source for migration', in A. Newman and S. W. Massil (eds.), *Patterns of Migration, 1860–1914: proceedings of the conference of the Jewish Historical Society and the Institute of Jewish Studies*, 1996), analysis of the dataset finds that 25 per cent of the district were locals and another 27 per cent were Londoners. Of the 18 per cent other British, in addition to some obvious port towns such as Plymouth, Devonport, Folkestone, Portsmouth and Harwich, places of birth given include: Birmingham, Cambridge, Cardiff, Cheltenham, Chesham, Essex, Guernsey and Manchester. As well as the obvious Irish and Jewish countries of origin, other places mentioned are South America, America, Canada and Germany.

12 Contemporary space syntax research by Bill Hillier and colleagues into urban layout and crime supports these conclusions. In a paper called 'Can streets be made safe?', he maintains that safer streets can be created by relatively minor changes to street layout, such as avoiding rear access points, making sure that public spaces are continuously aligned by building entrances and making sure that building entrances can be seen from each other. Such changes can have a measurable impact on natural surveillance and help to deter street crime. See B. Hillier, 'Can streets be made safe?', *Urban Design International*, 2004 9, pp. 31–45. Online http://eprints.ucl.ac.uk/archive/00001060/.

13 It is important to note that the classification of streets as red on the maps, ostensibly denoting a comfortable 'middle class' situation, masks a finer set of distinctions which can be found in the published statistics. It is likely that these streets were defined by Booth as Class G, a lower middle-class status which included occupations such as shopkeepers, clerks and some professionals. Indeed, according to the Booth notebooks, the street also included some workshops, including an employer of up to 200 at busy times.

14 C. Booth, 1886–1903. B351: pp. 104–5.

15 C. Booth, 1886–1903. B350: pp. 49–51.

16 D. Englander and R. O'Day (eds.), *Retrieved Riches: Social Investigation in Britain 1840–1914*, Ashgate, 1998 & 2003, p. 306.

17 A. Kershen, *Uniting the Tailors: Trade Unionism Amongst the Tailors of London and Leeds, 1870–1939*, Frank Cass & Co., 1995, p. 37.

18 See D. Rau, pp. 283–91.

19 C. Booth, 1886–1903. B351: pp. 100–1.

20 R. Evans, 'Rookeries and Model Dwellings: English housing reform and the moralities of private space' in Evans, R., *Translations from Drawing to Building and Other Essays*, Architectural Association, 1997.

21 J. White, *Rothschild Buildings: life in an East End tenement block 1887–1920*, 2003, pp. 29–30.

FURTHER READING

GENERAL WORKS

Place of publication is London unless otherwise given

Jack the Ripper

Begg, Paul, *Jack the Ripper: The Facts* (2004)

Begg, Paul, Fido, Martin and Skinner, Keith, *The Jack the Ripper A–Z* (1991 & 1996)

Curtis, Lewis Perry, *Jack the Ripper and the London Press* (New Haven, 2002)

Evans, Stewart P. and Skinner, Keith, *Jack the Ripper: Letters from Hell* (Stroud, 2001)

Evans, Stewart P. and Skinner, Keith, *The Ultimate Jack the Ripper Sourcebook* (2000)

Warwick, Alexandra and Willis, Martin (eds.), *Jack the Ripper: Media, Culture, History* (Manchester, 2007)

The East End

Fishman, William J., *East End 1888* (1988 & 2001)

Jones, Gareth Stedman, *Outcast London* (Oxford, 1971 & 1984)

Kershen, Anne, *Strangers, Aliens and Asians: Huguenots, Jews and Bangladeshis in Spitalfields 1660–2000* (2005)

Samuel, Raphael, *East End Underworld: Chapters in the Life of Arthur Harding* (1981)

Walkowitz, Judith R., *City of Dreadful Delight: Narratives of Sexual Danger in late-Victorian London* (1992)

White, Jerry, *Rothschild Buildings: Life in an East End Tenement Block 1887–1920* (1980 & 2003)

Wohl, Anthony S., *The Eternal Slum: Housing and Social Policy in Victorian London* (1977)

CHAPTER ONE

The imaginative geography of the Whitechapel murders
John Marriott

Work on the Whitechapel murders has been almost entirely devoted to wild speculation on the identity of 'Jack the Ripper'. Publication of this literature has become something of an industry for it attracts considerable attention; sadly, however, little qualifies as serious history. Having said that, Begg (2004) seems to open up this genre to new approaches since he is concerned less to identify the Ripper than to explore the social background of the myth. And the website www.casebook.org provides an extraordinary collection of primary written material. The best study of the media creation of the Ripper narrative is Walkowitz (1992) and this is nicely complemented by Curtis (2001) which usefully explores how the press operated at the time. The long historical background to the moral panic is detailed in two wonderful studies. M. Dorothy George, *London Life in the Eighteenth Century* (London, 1965), written some eighty years ago, has yet to be bettered, and Jones (1971) has effectively defined the agenda for more recent studies of the nineteenth-century East

End. More accessible are Fishman (1988), which is an entertaining social history of the people and conditions of the time, and White (2003) deals movingly with the housing reform provoked by the murders. An extensive collection of primary materials, John Marriott and Masaie Matsumura (eds.), *The Metropolitan Poor, 1795–1910* (1999), provides insight into how the poor were represented in the writings of evangelicals and social investigators.

CHAPTER TWO

The immigrant community of Whitechapel at the time of the Ripper murders
Anne J. Kershen

There are a number of books which provide a back-cloth to the Jewish presence in the East End of London in the latter quarter of the nineteenth century. These include the doyen of East End Jewish history, William J. (Bill) Fishman's *East End Jewish Radicals* (1975) and *East End 1888* (1988 and 2001). Others which set the scene are Todd Endelman, *The Jews of Britain 1650 to 2000* (2002), Lloyd Gartner, *The Jewish Immigrant in England 1870–1914* (1973), and the forerunner of them all, Charles Russell and Harry Lewis, *The Jew in London: A Study of Racial Character and Present-day Conditions* (1900). David Feldman, *Englishmen and Jews: Social Relations and Political Culture 1840–1914* (1994), locates the East End Jewish community within the contemporary political landscape, as do the early chapters of Geoffrey Alderman, *London Jewry and London Politics 1889–1986* (1989). Anne J. Kershen (2005) places the East End Jewish immigrant within the broader framework of 350 years of outsider settlement and compares and contrasts the migrant experiences.

The socio-economic and domestic environment of the Jews of the East End is explored in detail in

White (1980) whilst the largest employer of Jewish immigrant labour, the tailoring trade, is put under the microscope in Anne J. Kershen, *Uniting the Tailors* (1995), and Andrew Godley, *Jewish Entrepreneurship in London and New York 1890–1914* (2001). Gerry Black, *JFS The History of the Jews' Free School since 1732* (1998), and Sharman Kadish, *A Good Jew and an Englishman: The Jewish Lads' and Girls' Brigade 1895–1995* (1995), both detail the way in which the established Anglo-Jewish community sought to 'iron out the ghetto bends'. Anti-alienism and the consequent introduction of the 1905 Aliens Act, the first to control the entry of immigrants to Britain in peacetime, are examined in a selection of volumes; amongst these are Colin Holmes, *Anti-Semitism in British Society 1876–1939* (1979), John Garrard, *The English and Immigration 1880–1910* (1971), and Bernard Gainer, *The Alien Invasion: The Origin of the 1905 Aliens Act* (1972). Contemporary literature always provides a valuable insight into the life and times of its subjects and none more so than Israel Zangwill, *The Children of the Ghetto*, of which there are a number of editions.

CHAPTER THREE

Law, order and violence

Louise A. Jackson

There is a useful chapter on crime and punishment in Fishman (1988) while White (1980) contains many helpful insights. For further discussion of the experience of policing in this period, see H. Shpayer-Makov, *Making of a Policeman: a Social History of a Labour Force in Metropolitan London, 1829–1914* (2002). R. D. Storch, 'The Plague of Blue Locusts: Police Reform and Popular Resistance in Northern England 1840–57', *International Review of Social History*, 1975, XX, discusses the earlier role of the police in terms of class conflict. For policing as physical force, see Chapter 8 of C. Emsley, *Hard Men: Violence in England since 1750* (2005). For detailed accounts of the policing of prostitution, see S. Petrow, *Policing Morals: The Metropolitan Police and the Home Office 1870–1914* (Oxford, 1994) and J. R. Walkowitz, *Prostitution and Victorian Society: Women, Class and the State* (Cambridge, 1980). M. Fido and K. Skinner, *The Official Encyclopaedia of Scotland Yard* (1999), is a goldmine of useful information.

For information about London police courts see J. Davis, 'A Poor Man's System of Justice: the London Police Courts in the Second Half of the Nineteenth Century', *Historical Journal*, 1984, 27. M. Wiener, *Men of Blood. Violence, Manliness and Criminal Justice in Victorian England* (Cambridge, 2004),

discusses attempts to clamp down on male violence whilst L. Zedner, *Women, Crime and Custody in Victorian England* (Oxford, 1991), offers a valuable overview of the treatment of women within the system. The response of newspapers to the Whitechapel murders is analysed in Walkowitz (1992) and Curtis (2001). Finally, the myth of the 'underworld' is very usefully explored in H. Shore (2007), '"Undiscovered Country": towards a History of the Criminal "Underworld"', *Crimes and Misdemeanours; Deviance and the Law in Historical Perspective*, 2007, 1 (http://ccode.org/solon/Issue1.1.html).

In addition to court records and newspaper reports, a range of memoirs have been consulted such as Samuel (1981) and W. Goldman, *East End My Cradle* (1940). Magistrates' memoirs include C. Biron, *Without Prejudice. Impressions of Life and Law* (1936), M. Williams, *Round London: Down East and Up West* (1892), M. Williams, *Later Leaves* (London, 1893), and A. Magistrate (attributed to T. W. Saunders), *Metropolitan Police Court Jottings* (1882). Police memoirs include F. P. Wensley, *Detective Days: The Record of Forty-Two Years' Service in the Criminal Investigation Department* (1931), and B. Leeson, *Lost London: The Memoirs of an East End Detective* (1934).

CHAPTER FOUR

Common lodgings and 'furnished rooms': housing in 1880s Whitechapel

Richard Dennis

The standard history of philanthropic and state intervention in housing in Victorian London is Wohl (1977). Housing problems are also prominent in Jones (1984), a powerful interpretation of the problems of casual labour. Jim Yelling, *Slums and Slum Clearance in Victorian London* (1986), provides a thorough analysis of the costs, problems and impact of slum clearance, while White (2003) records the oral testimonies of some of the first inhabitants. Fishman (1988) has one chapter specifically devoted to housing, but housing issues permeate the whole book. Extensive use has been made of Lee Jackson's 'Dictionary of Victorian London' website, http://www.victorianlondon.org, which reproduces extracts and sometimes the entirety of many Victorian books and tracts. 'Casebook: Jack the Ripper', http://www.casebook.org/index.html, contains a massive archive of research (and speculation!) and very usefully reproduces countless contemporary newspaper articles, official transcripts, and reprints of modern

articles on Ripper themes. 'Charles Booth Online', http://booth.lse.ac.uk/, includes the police notebooks used to revise his poverty maps, while in Charles Booth, *Life and Labour of the People in London, First Series: Poverty* (London, 1902), Volume I deals with East End housing and Volume III with model dwellings. Other invaluable online sources include '*The Times* Digital Archive', http://gale.cengage.com/Times/index.htm, and 'Historical Directories', http://www.historicaldirectories.org/. The Census Enumerators' Returns for 1881 and 1891 contain useful information as well as the Medical Officer of Health's *Reports on the Sanitary Condition of the Whitechapel District* (in Tower Hamlets Local History Library), the Land Tax Assessments for Christ Church, Spitalfields (MS6008A in Guildhall Library), and the minute books and annual reports of the Peabody Trust and the Improved Industrial Dwellings Company (in London Metropolitan Archives).

CHAPTER FIVE

'Deeds of heroism': Whitechapel's ladies

Ellen Ross

Scholars in literature and history have explored the lives and writing of women 'slummers' in several interesting books. Some of these studies deal specifically with London, while others are organised around other themes. On London: Seth Koven, *Slumming: Sexual and Social Politics in Victorian*

London (Princeton, 2004); Deborah E. Nord, *Walking the Victorian Streets: Women, Representation, and the City* (Ithaca, 1995); and Walkowitz (1992). Ellen Ross, *Slum Travelers: Ladies and London Poverty, 1860–1920* (Berkeley, 2007), has an annotated anthology on the London poor by women writers, including several who are discussed in this chapter. Other excellent studies are: Anne Summers, *Female Lives, Moral States* (Newbury, Berks, 2000); and Frank Prochaska, *Women and Philanthropy in 19th Century England* (Oxford, 1990). One of the earliest, focusing on institutions (such as settlement houses) for single women, is Martha Vicinus, *Independent Women: Work and Community for Single Women 1850–1920* (Chicago, 1985).

Beatrice Potter (Webb) figures importantly in this chapter because of her published and unpublished accounts of her years living or working in Whitechapel. Deborah E. Nord explores her youth and East London years in *The Apprenticeship of Beatrice Webb* (Amherst, 1985) and a general biography is Carole Seymour-Jones, *Beatrice Webb: Woman of Conflict* (1992). Webb's own *My Apprenticeship* (Cambridge, 1926) is one of the best introductions to her early life. Also covering her East London years are the selections from her diaries edited by Norman and Jeanne MacKenzie, *The Diary of Beatrice Webb: Volume I, 1873–1892. Glitter Around and Darkness Within* (Cambridge, MA, 1982). Rosemary O'Day provides wonderful detail on Beatrice Potter's time in the Katherine Buildings, in 'How Families Lived Then; Katherine Buildings, East Smithfield. 1885–1890', in Michael Drake and Ruth Finnegan (eds.), *Sources and Methods for Family and Community*

Historians: A Handbook (New York, 1994), vol. 2. With a similar attention to local time and place, O'Day covers Potter's work for Booth in 'Before the Webbs: Beatrice Potter's Early Investigations for Charles Booth's Inquiry,' *History* 78, February 1993, no. 252.

Eleanor Marx was another important figure in East London history in the late 1880s and the 1890s. Her biographer is Yvonne Kapp, *Eleanor Marx*, 2 vols (New York, 1976). John Stokes has edited a collection of fascinating articles, *Eleanor Marx (1855–1898): Life, Work, Contacts* (Aldershot, Hants, 2000). Of special interest for this subject are the contributions of Lynne Hapgood and of Carolyn Steedman. The newest study of Marx is Sally Alexander, 'Eleanor Marx's Political Legacy – Self-Sacrifice or Self-Realisation?', *History Workshop*, 64, Autumn 2007.

Many of the other educated women in Whitechapel in 1888 now have their own biographies. Among these are: Anne Taylor, *Annie Besant: A Biography* (Oxford, 1992), and Joy Dixon, *Divine Feminine: Theosophy and Feminism in England* (Baltimore, 2001), also Liselotte Glage, *Clementina Black: A Study in Social History and Literature* (Heidelberg, 1981), and Deborah McDonald, *Clara Collet 1860–1848: An Educated Working Woman* (2004).

CHAPTER SIX

Mapping the East End labyrinth

Laura Vaughan

A good starting point for studying maps as a source of London's history is P. Whitfield, *London: a life in maps* (2007). See also the London Topographical Society's printed version of the Charles Booth maps

of 1889, which includes an illuminating introduction by D. Reeder (publication no. 130, 1984). Many other publications of the London Topographical Society are useful in this context, particularly the gazetteer and large-format maps, see G. W. Bacon, *The A to Z of Victorian London* (1987). On the internet, British History Online, http://www.british-history.ac.uk/, contains a digital library of many key sources of maps and books for urban history and historical geography.

The original Booth papers can be read at the London School of Economics and Political Science archive and online at http://booth.lse.ac.uk/. Edited extracts from his *Life and Labour of the People in London* can be found in H.W. Pfautz, *On the city: physical pattern and social structure; selected writings of Charles Booth* (Chicago, 1967). A review of the methods of Booth's study can be found in R. O'Day and D. Englander, *Mr. Charles Booth's Inquiry: life and labour of the people in London reconsidered* (1993).

In the field of urban history, the collection of papers by H.J. Dyos provides insight into the impact of urban development on life in the late nineteenth century, see *Exploring the Urban Past: Essays in urban history*, edited by D. Cannadine and D. Reeder (Cambridge, 1982). H. Carter's work, in particular *An Introduction to Urban Historical Geography* (1983), provides an important overview from medieval times onwards on this subject area. The most important starting point for space syntax analysis of the urban transformations wrought on London's housing is J. Hanson, 'Urban transformations: a history of design ideas', *Urban Design International*, 2000, 5, pp. 97–122, available online at http://eprints.ucl.ac.uk/

archive/00001397/. Other key texts on space syntax are the first book published in the field: B. Hillier and J. Hanson, *The Social Logic of Space* (1984), and the edited collection by B. Hillier, *Space is the Machine: a configurational theory of architecture* (Cambridge, 1996), available online at http://eprints.ucl.ac.uk/archive/00003881/. An interesting counterpoint to space syntax is the field of urban morphology and the work of M. P. Conzen is a good starting point – see 'Analytical Approaches to the Urban Landscape' in *Dimensions of Human Geography: Essays on Some Familiar and Neglected Themes* (Chicago, 1978), pp. 110–128.

The field of ethnic geography has burgeoned in the past 50 years, but some important starting points are C. Clarke, D. Ley and C. Peach (eds.), *Geography and Ethnic Pluralism* (1984). Other key texts are P. Jackson, *Race and Racism: Essays in Social Geography* (1987), pp. 254–75, as well as C. Peach, 'The Ghetto and the Ethnic Enclave', in *Desegregating the City: ghettos, enclaves and inequality*, edited by D. P. Varady (Albany, 2005), pp. 31–48. 'The ethnic geography of EthniCities: The "American model" and residential concentration in London', *Ethnicities*, 2, pp. 209–35, by R. Johnston, J. Forrest and M. Poulsen (2002), provides insight into the contemporary city, whilst a vital text on the geography of poverty is R. Lupton, *Poverty Street: The Dynamics of Neighbourhood Decline and Renewal* (Bristol, 2003).

INDEX

ACKNOWLEDGEMENTS

Credit must be given first to all the authors who have worked beyond the call of duty and produced text to tight deadlines. Lynda Nead and Judith Walkowitz were generous in their advice at an early stage of the project. As part of the museum team, Julia Hoffbrand, Robert Campbell and David Spence helped with the development of the book, Mike Seaborne and Anna Wright tracked down many rare images and Cathy Ross gave support and encouragement. The museum's photographers, Torla Evans, John Chase and Richard Stroud, cheerfully and professionally copied a vast array of material of which only a small proportion made it into the book. Laura Lewis and Sean Waterman helped to source images from other collections. Christian Beros-Contreros and Na'amah Hagiladi supplied the new maps. Peter Huddleston gave access to his wonderful collection of Goad maps that helped to inform a number of the book's chapters. Finally and above all, much credit lies with Peter Ward, the book's designer, who managed to keep everything under control and structured all the texts and images into a satisfying whole.

AW

PHOTOGRAPHIC CREDITS

All images are copyright the Museum of London except for the following reproduced by courtesy of

© The National Archives; p. 11; Plate 2
© Neptun-Film/The Kobal Collection; p. 14
© Tate, London 2008; p. 17 (bottom centre)
© Wm. B. Becker Collection/American Museum of Photography; Plate 1
© Royal London Hospital Archives; Plates 4–6
© Private collection; pp. 148, 262
© Peter Huddleston; p. 150
© The Peabody Trust; p. 153
Crown Copyright and Landmark Information Group Ltd; p. 159; Plate 13

© National Portrait Gallery, London; pp. 210, 216
© ADAGP, Paris and DACS, London 2007; p. 238
© BFI Stills; pp. 241, 259, 265
© Alan Moore and Eddie Campbell; pp. 242, 243
© Gainsborough/The Kobal Collection; pp. 244, 246
© BFI Stills – Canal+Image UK Ltd; pp. 245, 253
© Nero/The Kobal Collection; p. 247
© 20th Century Fox/The Kobal Collection/Jurgen Vollmer; pp. 249, 251
© BFI Stills – Granada International; pp. 254, 266
'Batman: Gotham by Gaslight' © 1989 DC Comics. All Rights Reserved. Used with permission; p. 257
© Hammer/The Kobal Collection; pp. 263, 264